FRAGMENTS
OF A
FADING MEMORY

LEN VEITZER

For
my son Jason, my precious Jason,
who left too soon

CONTENTS

IAN   JASON   MAIA   ELI   SETH

MY MOST ENDURING MEMORIES OF ALL:
THE ENTERING OF MY DEAR CHILDREN INTO MY LIFE

EARLY CHICAGO VIGNETTES

I couldn't have been more than three and a half. Whenever she could, my mother would go to the Sunday afternoon matinee performance of the Chicago Symphony Orchestra. She would usually find someone to baby-sit me but on this particular Sunday she wasn't able to. She really wanted to hear this program so she asked me if I wanted to go and I said "uh-<u>huh</u>!" because I loved to ride on the bus. We both got all dressed up, walked to the bus stop and boarded to go downtown. I sat next to the window on the right side and for me the ride was such fun because I could see all the buildings go by and all the cars in the street with us and all the people on the sidewalks. Then I would pretend I was driving the bus, rolling my arms as we made turns and mimicking the low engine growl as we started up from another stop. What fun it was to be the bus driver. Then suddenly, as I was driving down a wide boulevard, a very important looking building came into view. I knew it was important because there were two great stone lions flanking the broad stairway rising up to the entrance.

<u>Lions! Boy! That was really impressive</u>!

It was many, many years later that I came to know that that was the magnificent Art Institute of Chicago, *a revered place in the culture of this city. Also, many more years after that, I had occasion to be in Chicago and was riding down Michigan Avenue when suddenly, there it was again! Its two guardian lions spurring my memory to recall the experience I am describing here.*

We were ushered to our seats in the great hall. It was huge and filling up with people all around us. Our seats were on the right side of the left aisle and I settled into the first seat, my mom to my right. In front of us the musicians, all dressed up in fancy clothes, filled the big stage from side to side. Then the leader came out and everybody clapped. He stood by himself facing the musicians, his back to us. I was overwhelmed with the splendor of it all. And then they began to play and I was enveloped by music I had never heard before. When they were finished, the audience erupted with thunderous applause, I among them. Then they began another piece and I immediately felt so

1

fully connected. I leaned over and quietly asked my mom if she had a pencil. She produced a long fresh one from her purse and handed it to me. Unabashedly, I stepped out into the aisle and waving my pencil like a baton, began conducting, just like the man on the stage. People around us began to smile but to me it all seemed perfectly normal.

****

It was summertime in Chicago. I was about four years old and living with my parents in a large apartment building on Independence Boulevard on the West Side. One of my neighbors was a little girl about my age and we would often play together. One day we were running around the inner courtyard, gleefully chasing each other, playing tag. I was "it" but I just couldn't catch her. She was elusively swift and dodged and zigzagged out of my reach. She finally ran to a short stairway down into the basement, opened the door and ran in. I followed right behind her. We ran all over the basement but I still couldn't catch her. When she circled around and ran back out the door, she slammed it shut just as I got my hand on the doorknob. Now the upper half of the door was a thin glass pane and as the door slammed, it fell out and shattered onto my right arm. I had felt no pain so as I went up the stairs and reached out for the handrail, I was stopped in my tracks. My arm was covered with blood.

In a panic I ran up to my apartment on the third floor. My mother was frightened and wrapped a towel around my arm but was confused and didn't know what else to do. She knew nothing about tourniquet's or similar types of first aid. I would have bled to death waiting for an ambulance or in a taxi to the hospital. As good luck (or timing) would have it, it was now just after 12 o'clock and our fourth floor neighbor, the doctor, sometimes came home for lunch. We hastily ran upstairs and knocked frantically on the door. He was there! He quickly calmed everybody down, stopped the bleeding and stitched the two major lacerations on my tiny arm. I was told to rest for three or four days. As I lay on my bed trying to cope with my boredom, I did have a few visitors, including my playmate, whom I never did tag. My mom hired a high school girl to help look after me for the few days and I remember that she was pretty. That was nice.

2

****

Billy and I used to go to the movies on Saturday afternoons. I was about five years old and Billy, a neighborhood pal, was a year older. Billy knew his way around the area but I was totally helpless. So together we would cross the busy Independence Boulevard, walk another block and cross that street, then turn left and walk past an alley to the next corner. Another right and we would be at the box office in front of the theater. There was always a double feature and a cartoon. And the theater rocked with the screams and laughter and squeals of a couple hundred happy kids.

But I couldn't figure out how the images, even though in black and white, got up on the screen. My father, a fine and decent man, was a dedicated provider to the family, but he was incapable of providing guidance to the ways of the world, so I couldn't ask him. My beloved mother would not have had a clue. And so I learned a lasting lesson early on, even at that young age, that I had to try to figure things out myself. I didn't know anything about film or projection or how it all worked. Billy didn't know either and didn't care. Nor did any of the other kids around us. Left on my own with just my imagination and in spite of my ignorance, the best I could do was to deduce that the actors were live right behind the screen on some sort of a stage in back of the theater next to the alley, and with some sort of lighting or silhouette system the images found their way onto the screen.

So as soon as the movies were over I hurriedly urged Billy and practically dragged him out of the theater so we could quickly run around the corner and get to the alley to see the actors. But each time I would come away disappointed because they were always gone. I figured we had gotten there too late. We tried every week, but alas, failure, until by the end of the summer I had finally given up, still wondering.

LEN VEITZER
May 2014

OMAHA

Omaha, the largest city in Nebraska, had a population in the late 1930s of about 230,000, including about 10,000 Jewish residents. Meat production and agriculture, mainly corn, wheat and alfalfa, were the staples of the economy. The land was flat and featureless, there on the west bank of the muddy Missouri River, just across from the State of Iowa. Winters were brutally cold and summertime oppressively hot and humid. Summer thunderstorms were frequent and dramatic and winter's windy blizzards chilled to the bone. But it was a peaceful place, there were trees everywhere and the people open and friendly. And at eight years old I was going to live there during my most formative years.

But before my family and I moved to Omaha we lived in Los Angeles. And before that, Chicago, where I was born in 1930. My father had a grocery store on State Street on the South Side in the heart of the black neighborhood. We lived in an apartment on Independence Blvd on the West side, which then was a Jewish neighborhood. But because I was frequently sick with ear problems and my mother wanted a warmer climate, we moved in 1936 to Los Angeles. We lived in Boyle Heights and City Terrace in East L.A. In early September of 1937 my father took me out to a camp in Pomona for a week when my sister Natalie (Nanie) was born.

He had found work as a grocery clerk and as a butcher, and to be closer to his work we moved to Inglewood in the western part of the city. I loved it there. We were in a rented house in a quiet, semi-rural neighborhood. Every day was sunny and warm with flowers growing everywhere and birds flitting around and chirping in the trees. I was in the second grade and every morning my mother prepared a lunch box for me to take to school on the local school bus. And there was a small airport nearby and I would fantasize about flying in the planes that were buzzing about in the clear blue sky. Decades later that airport became LAX.

There was an empty lot next to our house and on the other side of the lot lived a little girl about my age. We liked each other and very much enjoyed playing together every day in the lot. Then one day she said, "My daddy says I can't play with you anymore."

"Why not?" I asked.

"Because you're a JEW."

My father was wearing out driving back and forth to his job in Long Beach and could not find anything closer. So my folks reluctantly decided to move back to Chicago. He would go first and when everything was set up we would follow. But on the way he stopped in Omaha to visit his brother Nathan, who persuaded him to buy a shuttered grocery store on 24th Street, the main avenue in the heart of the black neighborhood. And there my father opened Bernard's Market. It took a while but his hard work and growing reputation for honesty and fairness earned everyone's respect. He arranged for carrying accounts till payday on Saturday. And provided delivery service (me) to his older customers. I worked in the store on occasional Saturdays restocking shelves and delivering. Nathan and his wife Jenny had three children, Frances and Irving who were a little older than me, and Norman a little younger. They didn't live close by but whenever we could we would play together.

We were in a rented house on Decatur Street in Omaha's black neighborhood. I got beat up a lot. I was eight years old and was in Long Elementary School for 3rd and 4th grade. Becky Finer and I were the only white kids in the class. I was skinny and runty but could run like the wind, and I developed an avid interest in sports and competition.

We moved again and I spent the 5th grade at Kellom School. It was a year I enjoyed. Except for one day while practicing broad jumps in my front yard, a motorcycle roared by, and then a screeching of tires followed by the terrifying sound of a horrific crash. I rushed out to the street and saw the remains of the biker spread out all over the intersection. Riding on a motorcycle became an anathema to me.

We relocated again to 2047 19th Street and two years later a few doors away to 2029 19th Street. I was in the Lake Elementary School district. The school was evenly mixed between black and white students and I did very well in the 6th through 8th grades. I was 13 at my 8th grade graduation ceremony, which was directed by our exceptionally talented teacher, Mrs. Hornberger. It was 1943 and everyone in the whole class participated. Our class song was *"Summertime (and the livin' is easy...)"* from George Gershwin's 1935 opera *Porgy and Bess*. I was in an octet singing *Summertime* in four part harmony in pairs. All the other boys were black and my partner was Lorenzo Bean. And we were really, really good. In another part of the ceremony I recited the last few lines of the epic Rudyard Kipling poem *IF*:

"..... and--which is more--you'll be a MAN, my son!"

Everyone was amused, these final lines coming from a 79 pound, 4'-11" scrawny little runt.

On Saturday afternoons we all would go to the movies at the Corby Theater on 16th Street. There was always a double feature together with a weekly serial (10 weeks) and a cartoon. A free bag of popcorn with the beginning of each serial series. The theater was always packed with happy giggly kids. And it all cost a nickel!

When I was 12 years old I got a job after school setting pins in a bowling alley near downtown. Nothing was automatic then. The ball would come roaring down the alley and crash into the pins, scattering them into a pit. The setter (me) sat on the back ledge of the pit and as soon as the pins were down would leap into the pit and put them into a rack hovering above and send the ball back in the return trough. I was paid 7 cents a line. It wasn't much but I could bring back a couple bucks. Then about 7 or 8 o'clock I would take the streetcar home.

I used to collect stamps and lovingly kept them in a large album. There was a stamp store downtown and I would go there frequently to pore through the stamps for sale and sometimes buy a stamp or two. I also got into the terribly bad habit of stealing a stamp or two as well. My friend Irwin Ruderman would sometimes accompany to the stamp store, and he was aware of my larceny. Well, one day Irwin and I had big fight and he told my mother of the thefts and she told my father. He exploded with rage and angrily demanded that I bring him my precious album. He ferociously tore it to shreds and sent me to bed without dinner. I was devastated but the punishment was effective --- I never, ever stole anything again. And Ruderman and I were no longer friends.

At 13, as per custom, I had my Bar Mitzvah. Not the usual Saturday morning rite with Torah reading and speech and joyous celebration, but instead on a Thursday morning at 5 o'clock with a minion of ten men and only the Torah reading. It was a dark icy morning as my father and I walked the half mile to the shul. I did my ritual duty and 30 minutes later we walked back home. Why Thursday? First, because it's permitted and second, because Saturday being the busiest day at the grocery store my father couldn't (or wouldn't) afford to close for the morning.

I just loved airplanes. Not only to watch them fly around but also to watch them take off and land. When I was about 10 I started hitchhiking to the airport about five miles away from my house, out in the countryside, past Carter Lake. I would hang around for a couple hours, daydreaming about flying, and then hitchhike back. Just something I liked to do. One frigid winter day a pal and I couldn't catch a ride so we walked all the way to the airport, and when it was getting late we decided to leave. Carter Lake was frozen over so we thought we could save a lot of time by crossing over the lake. It was dumb and foolish but we made it across. Lucky!!!

I also began a hobby of building model airplanes. I could buy a kit for a dime, and with fast drying glue and a razor blade could fashion beautiful models of balsa framework and tissue paper covering. A thick rubber band down the middle of the plane when wound up would provide the needed propulsion for the model to fly! I reveled in the whole process and would spend hours and hours building these dozens of planes. But alas, after multiple flights and rough landings, some planes would become crippled, worn and sadly decrepit, and I felt it sorrowfully appropriate to provide a proper Götterdämmerung. I'd climb to the roof of our garage, and standing solemnly, wind the propeller, light a firecracker placed in the nose and launch the plane in its last noble flight.

I was 10 or 11 on one hot and lazy summer day as a couple pals and I had nothing else to do. And we were thirsty. A Coke or Pepsi would cost a nickel which none of us had so we decided to make our own pop. Well, how to do that. Of course I knew that pop was really <u>soda</u>

pop with fruity or similar flavoring so all we needed to do was gather the ingredients and mix them all together. So we started by walking around the nearby empty lot and picking up discarded pop bottles. And there were plenty. We washed them out with a hose and set them out in the sun to dry. Then in a big pot we made some flavored koolaid and when we added a couple spoonfuls of baking soda we couldn't figure out why the mixture didn't fizz. But no matter, we're going to make some pop! We filled three or four bottles with our mixture, found some bottle caps and pounded them on top. We offered them for sale to a few passersby but nobody was interested or thirsty enough. And I could not understand why they smiled while politely declining. And we were still thirsty. So now it was time to slake our thirst and drink some of our own hand made pop. We were so proud of what we had done that we made a little ritual of opening the bottles with great anticipation. I don't know why we never sampled our concoction before we offered it for sale but now was the moment of truth. We popped the tops and took hearty swigs. It was awful. It was worse than awful. We couldn't believe at how miserably we had failed. And it had all seemed so logically plausible.

So then a week or so later we thought we'd try smoking. Rolling your own cigarettes was a popular alternative in our low income neighborhood. In my father's grocery store we sold cans of loose tobacco and included free cigarette papers. So I found an empty Prince Albert can and we scoured the sidewalks and curb gutters for cigarette butts. I'd rip off the paper and empty the tobacco into the can. When the can was filled we hid behind a garage, and with free papers I had swiped from the store, we proceeded to roll our own cigarettes. We felt like big shots now. We all lit up and took our first drags. And coughed. And coughed and coughed. And couldn't get rid of the sour, god-awful taste in our mouths. Why would anybody want to do this, we wondered.

The Omaha school system was comprised of elementary school (kindergarten through eighth grade) and four years of high school. No junior high or middle school. Central High School was one of the top rated schools in the Midwest. It had an enrollment of about 1,200 students of diverse backgrounds. It drew from the poor neighborhoods as well as from the rich and the very rich areas.

Italians, Jews and black teens went to Central. Most students were white and there were no Hispanics or Asians. The classic four-story building was close to downtown at the corner of 20th and Dodge Streets. A streetcar line ran on 20th and through my neighborhood and was my regular means of transportation.

We moved again and this time my parents actually bought a house. 3018 Nicholas Street was about a mile farther west from where we had been on 19th Street. We lived there for about three years. It was two bus rides to Central High and in the winter, particularly with freezing sleet and deep snow, I still managed to slog to school, like everybody else. A "snow day" had not yet been invented in Omaha.

I had good grades and exceptionally fine teachers throughout high school. One of my favorites was the very sexy English teacher Virgene McBride. She would sit on the front edge of her desk, cross her shapely legs and conduct the class from there. She fueled many boys' adolescent fantasies and their big eyes and pubescent sighs were clearly palpable. She was a good teacher, gave intelligent assignments and knew the classics so very well. Everyone paid close attention and appreciated her dedication.

Another fine and memorable teacher was the legendary Frank Gulgard, portly and shaped like a penguin, who taught physics. He was affectionately called "Mr. G." He was kind of quirky with an irreverent sense of humor and gave many of his students aliases by which he called them. He had learned that I was dating a girl from Sioux City named Mona and I was quickly dubbed *"Mona's Friend."* And that's what he called me and how I had to label my tests and assignments. A couple months later when Mona and I broke up he gave me a middle initial and declared me to be *"Mona's X. Friend."* Everybody respected Mr. G and everyone paid attention because he was such an excellent teacher. On the last day of class before Christmas vacation he gave a pop quiz with about 10 questions. They were all pretty weird and everybody had trouble with them. Such as "What is heavier, a pound of gold or a pound feathers?" Nobody got that one right (feathers) because gold is measured in troy weight (1 pound =12 oz). I was totally stumped by all the questions and so I wrote *"God knows the answers to these questions, I sure don't. Merry Christmas."* When we all returned after the holidays we got our test papers back. Written on mine in Mr. G's scrawly hand was *"God gets 100, you get zero. Happy New Year."* He was one of a kind and we all loved him.

During the last two years of the war (WW2) and for two years after, I was in the ROTC and reached the rank of 1st Lieutenant. I was also on the staff of *The Register*, the school newspaper, for three semesters and sports editor during the last semester.

I liked girls and dated as often as I could, as long as there was another couple I could double date with. We didn't have a car in my family and I was totally dependent on my friends for transportation. I tried taking the streetcar a couple times with a date but that was too embarrassing. I envied my friends who had a car at their disposal and even if I didn't know how to drive, I desperately wanted one and the independence it would provide.

I enjoyed playing sports but because I was so small my activities were limited. I went out for football as a freshman in high school but got clobbered and took up wrestling instead. I made the team in the 85 pound class, the lightest available. I did well and won more matches than I lost. The next year I wrestled as a 95 pounder. I tried out for basketball but was too short. However, across the street from the high school was the Jewish Community Center (JCC). It was a marvelous facility with a well equipped gym, a running track and a large swimming pool. It was here where I played league basketball for several years. I was pretty good, fast and an accurate shooter. With an old beat-up ball we also played tackle football on grass in the park. We didn't have helmets or pads. And touch football in the street. Also in the street, after dark, we'd play "Kick the Can." On Sundays I played softball and sometimes baseball. I loved the sheer joy of competition. And I learned how to win with grace and lose with respect.

I was 15 when some friends took me to Rocket Recreation, a pool hall in downtown Omaha. Central High School was just four blocks from downtown so we went there frequently. That is where I learned to shoot pool. They also had a betting operation on baseball games. There was a big chalkboard on the wall with the day's games and the current scores. The system was to form a parlay by betting on the winners of two or more games. The more games (winners) selected the better the odds and the higher the payoff. The minimum bet was one dollar. The scorekeeper had a teletype machine that was always clacking and spitting out its tape with scores every half-inning of every game being played. And he would chalk them in on the big board. When making a bet he would write it on a receipt pad with a duplicate to the bettor. Everything was on a strictly cash basis. Of course it was all illegal but I could only guess how they did it. Although I bet a few times I mostly shot pool.

It was 1947 and in the late spring my parents announced to my sister and me that we are moving back to Los Angeles at the beginning of summer. They thoughtfully delayed leaving until after my high school graduation. They had sold the grocery store and the house and arranged to ship our furniture and belongings. We were packed and on the train the day after my graduation.

During that senior year I began dating a lovely girl named Rona Stein, who was a year behind me in school. She lived in an affluent neighborhood near Elmwood Park. We double-dated as often as I could make the arrangements. The romance had become very serious. But I was leaving and so we whispered our tearful goodbyes and promised to write.

After we moved to San Diego and I was a freshman at San Diego State, I missed Rona terribly. We began a loving correspondence, patiently, for the turnaround time was about 10 to 12 days. As our letters became more passionate I knew I was in love and must arrange to see her in the coming summer. In the late spring I needed to find a ride and hooked up with a fellow off the bulletin board who was driving to South Dakota. We left together right after finals and headed east. He did all the driving because I couldn't, and I paid for the gas. Three days later we were in Nebraska. I was so anxious to see Rona again, and hold her and kiss her and tell her how much I missed her. Yet the most peculiar and puzzling thoughts began to enter my mind. Sporadic thoughts, but fleetingly, that I was gradually a little less anxious to see her. What is going on here? Anyway, he dropped me off in Grand Island before heading north to South Dakota and I took a Greyhound bus the rest of the way to Omaha.

My folks had good friends in Omaha -- the Bondarins, and we arranged for me to stay with them for a few weeks. They were very gracious and welcoming and happy to see me. After settling in and having dinner with them, I took the two buses to Rona's house, a little nervous and unsure about how I really felt. Her folks were glad to see me and she was thrilled and as beautiful as I remembered. We were able to spend a happy and affectionate evening together before I had to leave to catch the last bus. This pattern continued for the next few weeks, except I didn't leave her house until very late and well after the last bus had gone. So I would walk the several blocks to Dodge Street and try hitching while walking the two miles toward 30th Street. Sometimes I got a ride and sometimes I didn't. Then I'd walk about a mile on 30th Street to the Bondarin's house, sometimes arriving around two o'clock in the morning. I did this almost every night for about five weeks. During this time I was able to resolve two major issues. First, a car will definitely be in my future, providing me freedom and independence. Once I have a car I will *never* let it go --- you can bet on that, I promised myself. And second, as my ardor toward Rona cooled, I realized that love can be illusory, a consequence of wanting to be in love.

I was starting to run low on cash so I decided to get a job to do some short time work. Not much was available but I heard that I might find something in the southern part of the city. South Omaha was largely industrial and the residential areas were mainly populated by people of Polish descent. I managed to get a job at the stockyards. Three streetcars each way got me there and back. Cattle were brought up from Texas and Oklahoma to Omaha and Chicago for slaughter and processing. Once here the steers were tightly confined in an acre of stockyards with holding pens and guidance chutes leading to the packinghouse, a very old 6-story industrial type brick building. Just inside the entrance opening each steer was conked on the head with a very heavy steel ball, rendering it unconscious. Its throat was slit and the carcass was laid out on the conveyer belt carrying it in for processing. I was assigned to the very hot and steamy second floor wheeling a cart full of warm and slimy innards to the elevator. Then up to the refrigerated fifth floor, reaching into the cart up to my elbows to unload the contents and return for another load. It wasn't physically demanding but the temperature differences between the two floors was worrisome. The smells throughout were almost overwhelming. Cafeteria style lunch was on the sixth floor on battered metal plates and with well worn flatware. When at 4:30 a bell clanged marking the last of the day's victims, everyone throughout the entire building loudly cheered. I did this for a week, got paid and didn't return.

I got another job in a brewery. I lasted there about a week also. One of the perks for working in a brewery was all the beer you could drink all day long. The men were all beer-bellied and as the day wore on more and more cordial. During the week that I was there was the semi-annual cleaning of the vats. The beer was all drained and the bottom cleaned of dead rats, clothes and all sorts of debris.

I had been in Omaha close to six weeks and it was time to go home. I visited Rona for the last time and we both agreed that our innocent romance had been a fine thing for each of us. I warmly thanked the Bondarins for their gracious and generous hospitality. Then, flooded with deep melancholy, I Greyhounded back to San Diego.

Although I didn't realize it until many years later, Omaha was a very good place to grow up.

LEN VEITZER
January 2018

MY BIKE HIKE

It was summertime in Omaha, I was 12 years old and I still didn't have a bicycle. In fact I didn't even know how to ride a bike. My father, as an incentive, promised he would buy me a bicycle if I got good grades in school. I received exceptionally fine grades, but my father reneged. It took a long time for me to get over my anger and bitter disappointment, but eventually I did.

Omaha in 1942 had a population of about 230,000 there in the middle of the country, but was not so far removed from the war. Rationing was in full force and War Bonds were widely promoted and sold. It was considered patriotic to buy a bond for $18.75 which would mature in ten years at $25. And there were blue stars hanging in many windows, representing a family member in the service. Sadly, some windows displayed a gold star for a son or husband killed in action.

I had joined the Boy Scouts a few months earlier --- Troop 62, and I was one of eight members in the Lightning Patrol. The troop would meet every two weeks and I would always look forward to taking the streetcar downtown to our meeting place at the Jewish Community Center. I began the merit badge program and soon had enough for my first advancement. We were also engaged in War Bond drives, and I would go from door-to-door selling Bonds. I really enjoyed all these activities --- they were stimulating and challenging and I felt I was doing my part.

One evening it was suggested within our patrol that we go on a bicycle hike. I loved the idea but with mixed emotions. I had no bike and couldn't ride one if I did. But a helpful fellow scout said he could arrange for me to borrow a bike from a friend of his. I was too embarrassed to admit that I didn't know how to ride but I was determined that I wanted to do this so I said OK. The bike was in my neighborhood so I went to get it and walked it home. All bicycles in those days were single speed with coaster brakes. They all had black balloon tires with red inner tubes. But not this one. Its tires were not black, but red! It looked goofy, like it was riding on its inner tubes.

I found a nearby parking lot and after about 20 minutes had learned to pedal, steer, slow down, stop, and most importantly, balance. Although I could barely reach the pedals I went out onto the street and with growing self-assuredness, rode around for about an hour exhilarated with my new skill and confidently knew I was good to go!

The following Friday morning my mom helped me pack up all my gear and provisions and I tied everything to the back of the bike. By late in the afternoon I was all set to go. There would be four of us and we would meet and spend the night at Dick Weintraub's house before leaving early Saturday morning. I was the youngest, two of the boys were 13 and Dick was 15. He knew his way around and had made all the arrangements for our camping site. I lived on 19th Street and Dick lived a few miles farther west on 55th Street. It was late afternoon as I pedaled about a mile to Dodge Street, the east-west artery that was also U.S. Highway 6 and known as the transcontinental Lincoln Highway. I got to Dick's house about six o'clock, weary, thirsty and hungry. We all had a fine dinner with the family and went to bed early. By eight the next morning we had had a hearty breakfast and were on our way. Back out to Dodge Street and westward past the city limits at 72nd Street. We were on the road, and with gas rationing, hardly a spot of traffic.

U.S. 6 was a two-lane highway that ran straight as an arrow through the Nebraska plains, over the low, undulating hills, flanked by cornfields and immense plots of wheat and alfalfa, before disappearing in the heat haze of the horizon so far, far ahead. After about five miles we passed Boys Town, Father Flanagan's home for "wayward boys" made famous in the 1938 film starring Spencer Tracy and Mickey Rooney. We continued on in tandem, just cruising along, and I was on the trailing bike. Suddenly my front wheel hit a crack in the pavement. The bike stopped, but I didn't. I shot out over the handlebars and landed face down on the highway. After skidding to a stop and being a little dazed, I got myself up, and except for a shredded t-shirt and a skinned nose, I was OK. The bike, my trusty red-tired companion, survived as well.

A little farther on we came across a four foot long rattlesnake, seemingly without a care in the world, wriggling on the highway right in front of us. None of us had been this close to snakes before, so we were curious and carefully looked him over. We decided to call him Charlie, for no particular reason. We were also concerned that he could get run over out in the roadway, so with a couple of sticks we were able to prod Charlie to the side of the road, and slipping one stick underneath was able to fling him well into the adjacent field, hoping he would stay there.

We had been on the road for a couple hours when Dick, who was in the lead bike, pointed ahead to the left toward a double gate along the fence line. We all turned off the highway, opened the gate and continued along a rutted dirt road for about a half mile up to the edge of the tree line. We were in a broad, lush meadow inhabited by about a dozen grazing heifers, while white butterflies flitted about among the wildflowers. This was perfect and where we would set up camp.

By now it was mid-morning and already getting hot. The air was humid as well, typical of Nebraska summers, and soon mosquitoes joined us, thirsting for fresh blood. We unloaded our gear and provisions, including plenty of water, and set up our two-man pup tents out in the open. We parked our bikes against some trees to be out of the sun and as everything seemed in order, we strapped on our small knapsacks and set out to hike through the woods. Dick knew what we were doing and where to go. There was no trail but we had a compass and marked our positions every 20 or 25 yards. After all we were Boy Scouts and we knew about that stuff.

Actually, it was especially pleasant walking through the forest of oaks and cottonwoods, the hackberrys and the black walnuts as the sunlight filtered through the canopy of their leaves above. After about half an hour we were out of the woods and approaching a small lake. The air was still and quiet as the heat and humidity closed in on us, punctuated only by the skritch of crickets and the trill of countless songbirds.

We couldn't resist the opportunity so we stripped naked and waded into the cool water, gooey mud squishing between our toes, then plunged all the way in, swimming and playing for about 15 or 20 minutes. We didn't have any towels with us so we just air dried and then got dressed. It was close to midday now so we sat on the ground in the shade of the nearby trees and dug into our knapsacks for the sandwiches that Dick's mother had prepared. We were really hungry and eagerly devoured them, as well as a bountiful bagful of fruits and vegetables.

Back at the campsite we played a little two-man touch football before resting awhile, and then began to make plans for the evening. Later in the afternoon we went into the woods and foraged for dead wood fallen from trees. One of us had brought an axe so we were able to cut proper sizes. Using wads of balled up newspaper, twigs for kindling and topped with criss-crossed logs we built a perfect campfire. And we had enough wood to last for hours.

Soon it was time for dinner. We had brought small chunks of beef cooled in an ice bag, and with onions, peppers, carrots, tomatoes and parsnips prepared several shish-kabob spears. We had whittled pointy ends on long thin shoots cut from the trees, impaled our kabobs and began to cook our feasts, juices bubbling and crackling over the open flames and enticing us with the most tantalizing aromas. Here we were -- four adventurous and happy teenagers now indulging our voracious appetites. We baked potatoes in a pit, munched celery sticks and bread, gorged on cookies and cake and washed it all down with pop. Now what could be better than that!

It gradually became dark as we sat around the roaring campfire, belching, telling dirty jokes, singing what few bawdy songs we knew and trying to imagine what girls' parts looked like. As the evening wore on we were all on the edge of exhaustion, but before we sacked out, we had to put out the fire. And of course we used the tried and true "Troop 62 Method." Standing back from the dwindling fire we peed on the embers with lofty, graceful arcs until the last wafts of smoke had disappeared. Now the meadow was black as pitch but the wondrous sky was ablaze with its overwhelming display of stars. We could identify the two Dippers, Cassiopeia, Orion, Cygnus, Virgo, Ursas Major and Minor and of course the North Star. Then to bed -- two to a tent. At first the eerie night noises kept me awake and wondering. But then I quickly faded and was out.

It must have been around five o'clock, still dark out, when we were all suddenly awakened by an unexpected sound. A tapping sound. At first softly and slowly, but soon louder and more rapidly.

IT'S RAINING!

In spite of our boy scout credentials, we were just not prepared for this. We all squiggled out of our sleeping bags and stuck our heads out the front of the tents, trying not to get too wet. We needed to talk about what to do next. In the morning we were going to slowly explore the natural flora and whatever critters we could come across.

Everything we had planned was going to be in the meadow and in the woods, but with this kind of weather, that just wasn't going to work. It was extremely disappointing so we decided to pack it up as quickly as possible and head home.

We had to scramble swiftly, relying on our flashlights to strike the tents, and managed to get everything folded, packed and stowed away just as morning light began to dawn. We took great care to thoroughly clean our campsite and leave it in the same pristine condition we had found it. But it was raining harder now, and without letup. We were getting soaked, but it was a warm rain and not altogether unpleasant. It was a long messy slog with our bikes through the muck back to the highway. We scraped the mud out of the spokes and off our shoes, mounted, and began the long wet journey back to Omaha. Happily, there was hardly any traffic. We were all pretty glum and didn't say much, just pedaled along, still being pelted by the steady summer rain, single file as before.

Until we got to where we had encountered Charlie. We stopped there to rest and wondered if he stayed in the field where we had left him or if he ventured back to the highway, and if he did, did he get across. Then we spotted what was left of him on the shoulder of the road. We were saddened by poor Charlie's bad luck, but lingered awhile and began to happily recall our experiences over the last 20 hours. These recollections so very much lifted our spirits and though soaked to the skin, we jumped back on our bikes and joyfully headed east and home.

It was almost eight o'clock when we clattered up Richard's driveway on 55th Street and sloshed into the house. Richard's folks had become a little concerned and so were glad to see us happy and intact. We changed into dry clothes and warmed up with some hot chocolate before enjoying a hot and hearty breakfast. We relaxed the rest of the morning and shared our experiences with Dick's parents. Well, most of them anyway. By noon the rain had stopped and it was time to give my thanks to the Weintraubs and to my mates and point my faithful red-tired companion back to 19th Street and home, all the while not knowing that this weekend would forever be embedded in my memory.

LEN VEITZER
June 2014

A SEA STORY

By the beginning of summer of 1949 I had just completed my second year of engineering studies at the University of California in Berkeley and was back in San Diego needing a summer job. I scoured the want ads in the daily newspaper fruitlessly until one morning I spotted something unusual and intriguing and maybe fitting my needs perfectly. It was for a summer position on an ocean research project for the Scripps Institution of Oceanography. I took the long bus ride out to La Jolla for an interview. And as the duties, schedules, pay and other details were clearly explained to me I grew more and more excited. I was  19 and this was going to be an unexpected and welcome adventure, as I had never been to sea before. I immediately signed on and was told to report the following Monday morning to the Scripps pier in La Jolla to embark on a two week research expedition on the R/V HORIZON.

This ship was built in 1944 as a Navy tug in WW2 and then given as surplus to Scripps in 1949. It was renamed the R/V HORIZON and carefully outfitted into a research vessel. Its length was 143', beam

33', range 7,000 miles and speed 13 knots. This voyage was going to be its first deployment in its new identity and the beginning of 19 years of yoeman service for Scripps.

The purpose of this study was to revive the fading sardine fishing industry by predicting where the best spawning environments would be the following year. It was part of the Marine Life Research Program, which studies the ecology of the waters off California, its currents, temperatures, chemistry, and their relation to the life in the waters.

The data gathering phase would be for two weeks starting off the central California coast at Morro Bay and out into the Pacific, stopping every 50 miles to take water samples, and at 300 miles out turning south for 50 miles, taking a sample and then turning eastward back toward the coast, again sampling at 50 mile intervals. Then we would turn south for 50 miles, and then again turn westward, sampling at every 50 mile stop. This would form a 50 by 50 mile grid, a pattern which we would continue as far as halfway down the Baja California peninsula before returning to San Diego.

The analytical phase was performed during the next two weeks on the second floor of a former Navy barracks in Pt. Loma, where I, among a couple dozen other workers using graphs and charts, crunched the numbers and correlated the information gathered at sea. This was 70 years ago and long before the convenience of computers, and so everything was done laboriously by hand. Although this work was tedious and boring, we were all able to provide very useful data. After this I again reported to the HORIZON for another two-week expedition repeating our sampling in the same areas we had done the month before. Then back to the Navy barracks in Pt. Loma again for two more weeks of analysis. What a lucky break this summer this was!

There were nine men aboard the HORIZON. The ship had a complement of the skipper and a three member crew including the cook. I was one of four technicians split into a pair of two man crews which would alternate shifts. There was also an oceanographer who manned the small laboratory. My partner's name was Miles and we coordinated well with each other. I understand he stayed on with the program and went on to a long career with Scripps. Although I got a little seasick on the second day out, by the next day I had quickly adapted and was fine and happy.

Depending on the winds and currents it took four to five hours to sail from station to station and about an hour to complete our work at each location. We worked around the clock, either in transit or stopped while taking samples. A small platform extended out about three feet from the deck on the starboard side of the fantail. At each station a boom and winch system would swing out and hover over the ocean next to the platform. A stainless steel cable, weighted on the bottom, would be lowered into the water. Six to twelve Nansen bottles would then be attached to the cable at 50 foot intervals and the entire assembly lowered to the desired depth, anywhere from 300 to 500 feet or more.

A Nansen bottle is a yellow-painted bronze cylindrical container used for taking samples of ocean water, several usually being lowered open on a line and each being closed at the desired depth by the action of a falling weight. The bottle is about 20" long x 2" diameter and is attached to the cable with a quick release mechanism at the top and a hinged attachment at the bottom. The cylinder is hollow inside and constantly open to the water around it as it is being lowered down with the cable. Attached to the outside of each bottle are three thermometers and another "messenger" hanging on the bottom. When everything is in order I send the first "messenger" down the cable. The "messenger" is a heavy solid bronze cylinder, about an inch in diameter and 4" long. It's not directly attached to the cable but fits around it and will slide down the cable and strike the top of the highest Nansen bottle. That impact releases the top of the bottle which then swings downward from its hinged bottom. This action closes the top and bottom valves on the bottle, trapping the water inside, and as the bottle flips, the attached thermometers trap their mercury at the temperature of the water. The "messenger" on the bottom of the bottle is also released and slides down the cable to the next bottle. This process is repeated until all the bottles have trapped their water and the temperatures fixed at their prescribed depths. Then they are carefully hauled up and removed one by one and taken to the small lab. The boom and winch are then retracted and secured in their regular place.

During this whole process the ship will drift due to wind and current. So it is important that that drift be measured. As soon as we arrive at a station, a long, weighted wooden pole with a rope attached to the top would be thrown overboard. The rope would have knots in it every six feet. The wood pole would remain upright and stationary where it was thrown into the water but as the boat gradually drifted, the rope would play out onto the sea. So after completing all our testing and all the bottles were in the lab, our last task would be to haul in the pole and coil the rope, counting the knots.

Both teams quickly became familiar with the various methods and procedures. All our samplings went smoothly and the processes, although still interesting, seemed to become routine. Cooperation came easily as did social interaction. Most of our hours were down time, sailing from station to station. And so we had great opportunity to engage in lengthy conversations about anything and everything. Sometimes the skipper would slow down to three or four knots so we could throw baited fishing lines over the fantail and troll, most often successfully, for something fresh for dinner.

But one night we were about a week out in what seemed like the middle of the Pacific Ocean. It was about two o'clock in the morning and my partner and I had the duty. It was a quiet, moonless night and the sea was deceptively calm. Aside from the single flood light atop the aft bulkhead illuminating the entire fantail, the sky and the sea beyond the deck were as one and were pitch black. When my partner Miles hauled the drift pole onto the deck he signaled the captain that it's OK to get under way. He then went back to the cabin while I was finishing up with the drift rope. The engine began to throb and we were soon slicing through the cold tranquil sea. The deck was a very bright spot in the middle of an ocean surrounded by darkness.

I was sitting against the aft bulkhead on an upside-down skiff coiling the rope and counting the knots. Then suddenly, out of nowhere, a gigantic rogue wave slammed into the starboard side of the ship and sent me flying ass over teakettle. In a flash I literally flew through the air toward the port side, my arms and legs flailing uncontrollably.

Until I was abruptly stopped in midair by the most
primitive of railings and absurd good fortune.

The railing on this ship was typical -- two cables, one about four feet high and the other about two feet high, with stanchions about eight feet apart. In an instant, as I hurtled headlong toward the ocean, the lower cable caught me under my right armpit. But the momentum swung my legs out under the cable and over the churning black sea. So there I lay, gazing straight down incredulously at the roiling inky water below me, my left butt firmly on the edge of the deck and my right arm tightly squeezing the cable. I felt safe and secure enough for the moment, so I paused for several seconds to marvel and contemplate just how close that was. The skiff was gone and I almost followed right after it, swallowed into the black night. I was alone on the deck and had I gone overboard, I wouldn't have been missed for hours.

And I still think of how random chance, just pure damn luck, ruled my night.

LEN VEITZER
May 2014

THE ARMY YEARS, 1952-1954
PART 1

FORT ORD
Induction

I had registered with the Selective Service System in September, 1948 as required by law when I turned 18 and was attending college. Four years later in late August of 1952 I received my draft notice. I had been doing very well in my classes at Berkeley and was preparing to begin my third year in the School of Architecture. It was the second year of the Korean War (euphemistically called a "police action"). My plans for school were going well --- the war was not. Too little progress and too many casualties every day.

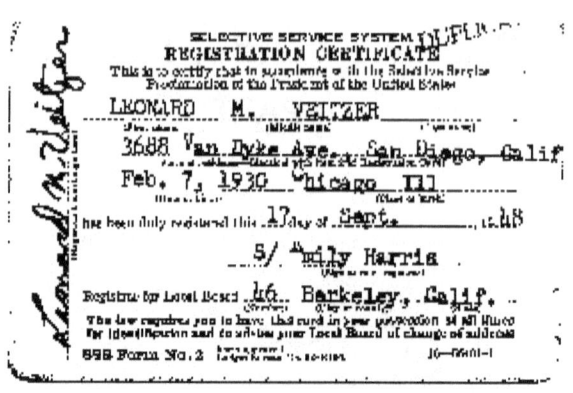

All along I had been applying for and receiving student deferments (I had spent my freshman year at San Diego State College as an engineering major, then at Cal the next year in engineering before changing to architecture where I continued for two more years). When I applied for a continued deferment, I was told that college deferments are only for four years and that I had already been deferred for four years. Unhappy but resigned, I applied to the University for and was granted a leave of absence for the duration of my service.

I was staying temporarily at the fraternity house and my old '36 Buick sedan (without a grille) for which I paid $35 was parked across the street. I always tried to park it there because the street sloped and the battery was dead and I'd be able to coast downhill to get it started. Well, I had no idea if I'd ever be back to see that car again, so I just left it there. I gave the keys and the pink slip to someone in the house. Years later I was told that little by little the car got nudged forward until it ended up in the intersection. The police had it towed and looked but couldn't find me.

So "..... report to the Greyhound Bus Depot in downtown San Diego at 8:00 a.m. on October 22, 1952." I was 22 years old and wondering if I would ever get to 23 or 24 or 25. As I tearfully kissed my folks and sister goodbye that early morning, they must have wondered if they would ever see me again. Only after I was a parent myself could I fully realize what fear and anxiety they must have been feeling.

I had very mixed feelings about going to war. Naturally there was the serious risk of death or maiming. Also the notion of killing someone was particularly troublesome. And I really didn't want to go - - I had other important things to do. However there was never, never any thought of dodging the draft. My strong sense of obligation as a responsible citizen compelled me to accept the circumstances without whining or conniving, to do my duty and to try to make the best of it.

The bus was full as we motored north for most of the day to Fort Ord on the Pacific coast, several miles north of Monterey. Disembarking amid a kind of organized chaos with scores of draftees from all over the state, and directed to this place and that and solemnly getting sworn in, I was now a soldier in the U.S. Army, serial number US56109049. Two days later, after IQ and aptitude tests, medical exams and shots, uniforms, orientations, rules and lots of additional testing, this large batch of raw recruits was ready for assignment to Basic Training camps.

Did I mention that I've always benefited from unusual "good luck" in major events affecting my life?" Some call it "good timing" or "serendipity", but no matter. Almost all basic training is for infantrymen, the dog-faced, mud-plodding cannon fodder. Fort Ord is an infantry training camp. However, a call comes in every eighth week for a detachment of new recruits to be sent to Fort Bliss in El Paso, Texas for <u>artillery</u> basic training. This was one of those weeks and twenty or so were called out to go to Texas, I among them. Another was a fellow from El Cajon I seemed to get along with pretty well, name of Roy Wieghorst.

FORT BLISS
Basic Training

Fort Bliss is a sprawling army artillery base on the outskirts of El Paso. In one outlying section is where recruits from all over the country undergo sixteen weeks of basic training. "Recruits" include draftees and regular army (RA) enlistees. At the end of basic training Recruits are promoted to "Private." Artillery includes heavy weapons from large cannons to anti-aircraft as well as the electronics to control these systems.

Every new soldier is assigned a Military Occupation Specialty (MOS) based on civilian experience, initial testing, tactical needs, and some unfathomable military logic. Although my background included design and construction, I was assigned, in typical Army fashion, an MOS 1725 for anti-aircraft fire control, the electronic aiming (control) of the big guns to shoot down enemy aircraft. The first eight weeks of becoming soldiers is the same for all recruits, but with some additional emphasis on each man's MOS. The second eight weeks is devoted to intensified instruction in each trainee's specialty.

The Basic Training part of the camp has the usual array of administrative and classroom buildings, mess halls, PX, parade grounds, etc. Troops were accommodated in 5-man tents and were assigned alphabetically. My tent-mates were Valdivia, Vasquez, Vega and Villalobos. I felt alien and invisible because Spanish was spoken exclusively. In the tent next door my new friend Wieghorst was quartered with the hoodlum Wiegert brothers, Wagers and Velasquez. We all decided to take our chances and arranged a tent swap of Velasquez and me without going through channels. It seemed like a good idea and no one else was ever any wiser.

Our leader was a Sergeant Betts, a tough black career soldier who had rotated back from Korea and knew what we needed to know. He was good and very strict, but he was fair. And he liked to say "I will fly, I will float and I will run, but I do not walk. And when I run, you will run." He cared about our survival and wanted to make good soldiers out of this ragtag bunch. Betts was supervised by a weary looking second lieutenant who seldom appeared.

My first (and last) stupid mistake occurred on about the third or fourth day. Reveille was at 0500, formation at 0530 and then a march to the mess hall for breakfast. It's cafeteria style and by the time I got to the servers most of the food was already gone. At the after-breakfast formation the lieutenant asked if everyone enjoyed breakfast, and I, believing that things ought to be done right, spoke up. Well, when the formation was dismissed, he marched me back to the mess hall and ordered the cooks to give me food. They did, all right, and plenty of it. And in the army, it's "take all you want but eat all you take." When I left the mess hall, I thought I would explode. After that, servers glowered at me when I passed through but I always got enough to eat. And I learned that irrespective of what's right and what's wrong, in the Army at least, it's prudent to know when to keep your mouth shut.

My new constant friend became the Garand M2 30-caliber semi-automatic 9½ pound rifle. It seems we went everywhere together. We became so intimate that I memorized all its parts and disassembled and cleaned it every day. I even learned how to disassemble and reassemble it in the dark. We would spend many enjoyable hours on the firing range, always improving our marksmanship. It was right there on my shoulder alongside my 30 pound pack during five, ten and fifteen mile marches. We really bonded.

On Monday morning of our sixth week we marched twelve miles with full 45 pound pack and rifle to bivouac at what is called the "chicken ranch." It's right out in the middle of the desert where sand and dust is six inches deep. It's hot in the daytime and freezing cold at night. We slept in sleeping bags in two-man tents, ate out of mess kits, ran through tactical night problems, dug foxholes, crawled on our bellies under live machine gun fire, and just about everything else a soldier does in the field. We marched back to base on Friday, worn and grimy but glad to be back. The next morning we all marched in a parade. Then the Ss, Ts, Us and Vs were picked for guard duty, which I had to stand till 0930 Sunday morning.

Roy and I developed what became a bonded friendship. We really became buddies. After dinner we'd go to the PX, a smoky and boisterous place, with country western music blaring from the juke box. It was there that I developed an anathema to country western, although in recent years I have mellowed. We were restricted to base for the first eight weeks, but during the second eight weeks weekend passes were available from noon Saturday to reveille Monday morning, but no farther than El Paso.

And so we were among the hundreds of GIs that flooded the streets of downtown El Paso looking for some relief from the rigors of army life. We discovered that counties in Texas had their own rules about selling alcohol and in El Paso you couldn't buy a mixed drink in a bar. But you could bring in your own bottle and order a 'set-up', which was a glass with ice and a bottle of mix. A little awkward but we managed. It turns out that an officer on the base, Col. 'Jimmy,' was a friend of Roy's father Olaf and arranged for Roy to get a long weekend pass. Roy flew to San Diego, picked up his car and his own civilian clothes as well as some of mine from my folks' house, and drove back to Fort Bliss Sunday. You see, Roy and I had a plan. We would load up the trunk with liquor and mix and have our own bar. We'd pick up chicks and have a real good time. Ha! Never worked out that way. Wonder why. Ahh, the follies of naïve youthful optimism. But the car was a welcome ticket to short bursts of freedom. Against the rules one weekend we drove to Las Cruces, NM for a double date with two lovely young ladies. I can't recall how that was arranged but they directed us to a Mexican restaurant that looked like a rundown shack. But once inside it was like a beautiful hacienda. We all had a fine time and Roy and drove back that night. Another Saturday afternoon we ventured out to the Carlsbad Caverns.

 It too was farther than we were allowed to go but we figured we'd be anonymous in our civvies and no one from Fort Bliss who would know us would likely be there. Ha

again! Half way through the caverns we spotted Sgt. Betts off in the distance in amongst the large crowd. We were mindful of fellow recruits Krantz and Kravitz, who over the Thanksgiving weekend thought they could get away by slipping out and flying to San Diego. They got caught and were seriously disciplined. So we took appropriate evasive action, and on high alert, managed to avoid Betts and enjoy the caverns.

Roy's MOS was 1514 as a radar operator, an integral part of the anti-aircraft system. I felt that that would be much more preferable for a number of reasons, but I hadn't qualified high enough on the electricity proficiency tests at Fort Ord. I needed to find a way to make a change.

It so happened that the Colonel in charge of basic training somehow learned that I knew how to design and draw, and he needed someone to make signs. So he set me up at a desk in his office and set me to work a couple hours a day. My work was exceptionally good and he was very pleased. One day he asked about my training and I told him that although it was going fine, I hadn't qualified for the radar MOS and was confident I could do well if given the opportunity to retake the test. He arranged it for the following week. I then spent every available hour at the camp library boning up on electricity. I passed the test and the Colonel arranged a change in my MOS to 1514. Man, was I happy. I went on to complete basic training as a radar operator and was subsequently promoted to Private in the U.S. Army and now earning $78 per month. [multiply by 8 to equal 2013 dollars]

On 21 Feb 53, our final day at Fort Bliss, the transformation in three and a half months of a motley group of apprehensive civilians from every background into capable, proud, disciplined men was clearly apparent and quite remarkable. Now everyone's gear was packed into their duffel bags as we fell into formation. The air was electric with speculation and hope, because each man was about to get new deployment orders, either to the Far East, Europe or stay Stateside. And nobody wanted Far East Command – that's where the war was.

Roy and I used to fantasize about April in Paris and traipsing all around Europe having the times of our lives. We could almost taste it. The harsh reality turned out to be that I, together with 90% of the others, was ordered to report to Fort Lewis, Washington on 9 March

53, to await transport to Korea. Several troops went to Europe and a few stayed Stateside. Roy remained as an instructor at Fort Bliss but months later was transferred to Germany. We all said our farewells and good lucks, but were still keenly aware of the unspoken -- that some of us would die.

> *Roy and I became fast friends and still get together about once a month for lunch. I designed my first San Diego house for him and Barbara in El Cajon in 1960, and a second one in southern Arizona in 1989.*

And that afternoon Roy and I drove back to San Diego in his car for a very welcome two week furlough. My folks and my 16 year old sister Nanie were overjoyed to see me and I chose to spend most of the time at home with them. Mom had been wanting for a long time to go to Israel to see her beloved sisters Gita and Sarah, brother Reuven, assorted nieces and nephews, as well as her mother's gravesite. But she just wasn't able to afford it. And I was heading into a war zone not knowing if I would ever be back, so I withdrew all my savings and gave it to her, saying only "stay as long as you want." I had just turned 23 a couple weeks earlier.

FORT LEWIS
Deployment to Korea

I arrived at Fort Lewis, a huge army base between Tacoma and Seattle, Washington, on 9 March 53. The base is a major

embarkation point for transport of personnel to the Far East. Several thousand troops are assembled waiting for shipping orders and otherwise have nothing to do. So of course the army finds busy work – KP, picking up trash, painting rocks, anything to keep the men occupied. But we did get weekend passes. On the first weekend Shelly Brown from L.A., whom I knew at Fort Bliss, and I took the bus to Seattle and headed straight to the University of Washington campus. Why? Because there was a Sigma Alpha Mu (Sammy) fraternity house there and I could always depend on the gracious hospitality of my fraternity brothers. We were warmly received and though still in uniform, made to feel a little civilian again. The war still raged and everyone knew where we were going. There was a party at the house that night and we met some nice young women. We stayed overnight, toured the campus on Sunday and returned to camp that evening. This made the following week of tedium a little more tolerable.

There were huge formations every morning and at times names would be called out for the bus ride to Seattle to board a troopship. No one knew when they might be called, so every morning anxieties were high. And in an information vacuum rumors were rampant. This almost surreal existence for me went on for three more weeks. The bright spot however was that as each weekend approached we could plan to go back to Seattle.

And that we did – every weekend to welcoming accommodations at the Sammy house. On one of those Saturday nights we were astonished to learn that they had fixed us up with dates! And even lent us a car for the evening! Can you believe that? We picked up our dates and decided to go to a movie in downtown Seattle. We got there about an hour early and decided to have a drink in a cocktail lounge across the street. It was crowded but we did find a small round table and people around us smiled and seemed congenial. We settled in and ordered. I was used to the disdain, at least in those days at home, that locals showed the many sailors that had a few hours of leave in San Diego. And here we were in uniform in Seattle, our Fourth Army shoulder patches from elsewhere indicating we were in transit, a clear message. The waitress brought our drinks and when Shelly and I each reached into our pockets for our wallets, she smiled and nodded over toward an elderly couple sitting at a nearby table and said, "They were honored to buy your drinks, and wished you both the very best of luck."

> *Every time I tell this story I can't help but tear up. And although I've never been back to Seattle, it is still one of my favorite cities.*

In the middle of the third week, Shelly's name was called and he shipped out. I went to the Sammy house in Seattle that Saturday and with several others had a fine time at a sorority house party. The next day the weather had turned cold and rainy, reflecting my mood, as I returned to Camp and back to the dreary routine.

On 7 April 53 I received my shipping orders, rode the bus to Seattle and boarded the troopship USNS Gen. R.L. Howze. I was one among 3,000 soldiers, all Privates, except for about a dozen Corporals and a handful of Officers. Our destination was Yokohama and would take about 15 days, much longer than for a normal crossing. Our ship had charted a zigzag course so as to avoid Russian submarines.

WESTWARD ON THE PACIFIC
The Crossing

You can't have 3,000 restless men just lolling about the ship for a couple of weeks. So one third were assigned to KP, one third to guard duty and one third to cleaning up the ship. These duties were rotated every three days. Once the ship was underway and duties assigned, the loudspeaker blared into action with announcements of all kind.

One in particular struck my ear. "Anyone interested in producing the ship's newspaper report to the chaplain's office at 1400 hours." I was there a half hour early and was hired on the spot to produce the artwork, headlines and graphics. There were three other "reporters" including one Charlie Justice who had been at CBS in New York. We became buddies, looking after each other. The unbelievable and unexpected benefit was that we were assigned to this office to produce this paper and were

relieved of all other shipboard duties. So we put out the paper every morning while enjoying our coffee and cakes, strolled the decks for awhile, had lunch, returned to the office for more coffee and banter,
    walked about again and stretched out the afternoon till dinner. Our
    tools were an old fashioned mimeograph machine, old typewriters using purple mimeograph paper, and a stylus that I used to cut the artwork and headlines into the paper. We really did pretty good work and were highly commended by the troops, the chaplain and the Navy brass. Also, in recognition for our worthy contribution to the ship's morale, we were each awarded a special Certificate, "The Order of the Golden Dragon" for crossing the International Dateline on 17 April 53, signed by the Commanding Officer and Neptunus Rex. This is what I did for fifteen days.

    Sleeping quarters on ships, always below decks, are densely packed. The bunks are like hammocks but with canvas stretched tightly in a metal frame. They are stacked one above the other about 18" apart. I selected the topmost bunk because you could barely see it from the floor. In addition, there was a duct that passed across the bunk, obscuring it even more. I could barely roll over. When reveille sounded at 0500 everyone scrambled out of their bunks, dressed, went to the head and then off to breakfast. That is, everybody but me. Nobody saw me as I dozed away. I finally clambered down about 0600 while everyone was gone. I washed and dressed and still made it on time for breakfast. Then on to "work" at the paper. And I was able to manage this caper for the whole trip.

A few men got seasick after we left Seattle but that passed after a day or two. Heading toward a war zone, the general mood on the ship was serious and somber. Many men were seen in prayer. To relieve the tension there were movies every night and occasional bingo. Others read books from the ship's library or played cards or shot craps. There were no fistfights or incidents, as discipline was very well maintained.

CAMP DRAKE
Preparation for War

We arrived at the U.S. Army Port in Yokohama, on 23 April 53 and were immediately hustled onto a train standing by at dockside. Yokohama is about 20 miles south of Tokyo on the eastern coast of Honshu, the largest and most populous in the Japanese chain of islands. An hour and a half later we spilled out of our train, fully packed duffel bags on our shoulders, onto the rail yard of Camp Drake, then by buses to the main campground.

Camp Drake is just northwest of Tokyo and is devoted only to processing incoming and outgoing troops. It is run like an extremely efficient machine. The trains, the buses and the troopships in Yokohama are constantly in action.

We were assigned barracks to sleep in but were told we wouldn't get much sleep anyway because there is much processing to do and the turn-around time is 36 hours. So in a day and a half we (all 3,000 of us) had countless orientations, exchanged our money (greenbacks) for scrip, had many inoculations, were issued helmets, rifles and bayonets, signed insurance documents and next-of-kin instructions. We went out to the firing range and zeroed-in our rifles. We were fitted with combat clothing and equipment. Of course we ate, wrote letters, and many prayed.

Late in the afternoon of the second day the final full formation of all the troops was called. The commander read off a list of 80 names and ordered these men to fall out and go to Building so-and-so. I was among them. We all assembled in the building, very concerned and wondering why we were there. A lieutenant entered and told us that we had been selected to go to various schools for advanced training. You could hear a pin drop. He also said it wasn't mandatory but no one, I mean no one, opted out. He then read off the assignments and handed out the individual orders.

All the schools in the Far East Command were located on Eta Jima, a small, self-contained island off the east coast of Honshu. That is, all the schools but one. That one is at the Headquarters of the 40th Anti-Aircraft Artillery Brigade, (AAA), about half way between Tokyo and Yokohama, and is the headquarters of all the anti-aircraft units in the Far East Command. And that is where I was assigned to the Far East AAA Specialist School, together with six other men.

Then the 80 of us were marched to the armory to turn in our weapons and combat gear. As we returned to our barracks to get some much needed rest and relief, we passed the large group of our shipmates, all 2,920 of them, loading onto buses to take them to the train to take them to Yokohama to reboard the USNS Gen. R.L. Howze to take them to Pusan, South Korea.

Several weeks later I learned that Shelly Brown, my buddy from Fort Bliss and Seattle, had been killed in action.

JAPAN
Advanced Training

The Far East AAA Specialist School was at the headquarters of the 40th Anti-Aircraft Brigade along an inland road and rail line connecting Tokyo and Yokohama. It was in a rural area with small farms and houses and situated between Hiyoshi and Motosumiyoshi, two small towns that served the countryside. Their streets were unpaved and dusty except when it rained and became muddy and sloppy. Most people would walk in elevated wooden shoes called *geta*. Most women wore kimonos and men would be in some type of work clothes.

Occasionally a man carrying two buckets balanced on a long pole across his shoulders would walk by at a brisk pace, his back stooped. His burden was known as "honeybuckets" and contained reeking manure from livestock and domestic outhouses. He would sell this as fertilizer to farmers. Sometimes a larger load would be hauled in an ox-drawn cart. Nonetheless, these were charming little villages with many children and very friendly people.

The camp itself, a former Japanese Officer Training School, was about ten acres within a perimeter chain link fence. Two three-story concrete buildings dominated the site and served as the headquarters and administrative offices for all anti-aircraft artillery units in Japan, Korea, Okinawa and Guam. It was commanded by a Brigadier General. The base was bisected by a central street from the front gate to the rear of the site. The camp accommodated about 150 men in several one-story barracks buildings. There were six classroom buildings, also single story, and outdoor instructional equipment, such as radar/computer trucks and vans, 90 mm anti-aircraft guns, 40 mm ack-ack light cannons and 50 caliber machine guns, generators and fuel and vehicle storage. The large mess hall also served as a movie theater, and a PX (Post Exchange) and Army Service Club provided services and after hours recreation. A small chapel, a guardhouse, a dispensary, a swimming pool and miscellaneous service buildings enclosed an extensive open area used for formations, inspections and morning calisthenics.

There were always ongoing classes as students would be drawn from incoming personnel like myself and from existing units stationed all over the Command. Classes varied from three to eight weeks after which students would return to their units or be reassigned. First formation would be after breakfast at 0730 and classes would begin at 0800 hours. After an hour break for lunch classes would resume until 1600 hours. Then everybody was off until the next morning. With only morning classes on Saturday and no classes on Sunday, we could get passes for the weekend until roll call Monday morning.

It was 27 April 53 and I was assigned to a six-week course for more advanced training of that which I had received at Fort Bliss. In addition to the six others assigned with me at Camp Drake, there were eleven or twelve men from units all over the Far East sent here to receive additional training. The non-com instructors were good and followed their lesson plans efficiently. We spent a lot of time practicing in the outside equipment – trucks and vans that contained the electronics.

This was World War 2 equipment, the best technology currently available. The main element was a semi-trailer van solidly packed with electronics. Connected to the trailer with long cables were several 90 mm anti-aircraft guns. This was in the days before transistors, microchips, circuit boards and nanotechnology. This was our computer and we had to contend with resistors, capacitors, temperamental vacuum tubes and miles of wiring. Any replacements were hand-soldered. The output circuits of the vacuum tubes needed frequent readjustment because the tubes produced a lot of heat and the data would fluctuate. Constant vigilance was required to keep the dozens of dials reading right. This technology is what I was originally trained for before I transferred to radar.

Searching the sky from atop the van was a rotating six-foot diameter parabolic radar antenna. Information gathered by the antenna would be fed to the computer below. Inside the front end of the van was the radar scope and its array of controls. The radar operator (me) would sit there and look for blips on the 8" screen as the scanner would sweep in circles following the rotating antenna. A blip represented something significant in the sky, usually an airplane, and in wartime presumed to be an enemy bomber.

The mathematical problem was to fire a projectile from the ground that would intersect and explode at a point in space exactly where the moving target is predicted to be. A little like a forward pass to a racing receiver, except the ball doesn't explode when it gets there.

And here's how it was done. The radar operator is constantly focused on the sweeping scan on the screen. When a blip appears, indicating that a plane is reflecting back the radar signal, the operator locks onto the blip. The radar stops rotating and follows the target. This information is fed into the computer as direction, altitude and speed. The computer calculates where to aim to gun and how many seconds are automatically cranked into the fuse when the shell is loaded. The presumption has always been that bombers must travel in a straight line on a bombing run. As far as I know, no bombers were detected in Korea because the North Koreans didn't have any bombers. So the anti-aircraft guns were deployed on the front lines as field artillery firing horizontally at enemy lines. My initial training at Fort Bliss before transferring to radar was as a computer operator, so now I was proficient at both. It's interesting to note that the computations performed in that huge van could now be handled in a small hand-held, properly programmed electronic device.

The barracks was a single-story wooden building with ten beds on each outside wall and a wide aisle down the middle. At one end was the latrine and showers. Once I settled in my quarters I picked up a little Japanese dictionary and phrase book. I wanted to learn the most important words and phrases – expressions of courtesy, numbers, days of the week, directions to this and that, and so on. And subsequently, with use I would pick up more vocabulary. Ultimately, communication was pretty manageable, using some of my primitive Japanese, their tentative English and quick sketches with pencil and paper.

The first Saturday afternoon, I walked about a half mile to Moto-sumiyoshi just to explore and see what a small Japanese village was like. Almost all structures were single-story wooden buildings packed tightly against one another. A random mixture of shops, services and houses. Folks were busily shopping for vegetables, rice, poultry and pastries. And there were knots of women bustling about and chattering away, as well as students on their way to or from school. Very much like small towns everywhere on a Saturday morning. I was not a curiosity walking down the main street because they were used to seeing Americans there.

On Sunday, I walked with fellow classmates Thad Kelley and Rod Reppe up to Hiyoshi and took the 25 minute train ride north to explore Tokyo. We were in the central area of the city and I remember well my first impressions on that beautiful clear, Spring day. The famed cherry trees were everywhere and in full blossom. It was truly breathtaking. The streets were noisy and congested with so many people walking so fast and cars and taxis jockeying for right-of-way, horns blaring. Large sections of Tokyo had been flattened and burned toward the end of the war but remnants of the devastation were nowhere to be seen.

Streets, buildings and houses had been rebuilt and one would never know that death and destruction had been so widespread. When the war ended less than eight years earlier, people were fearful and apprehensive, not knowing what to expect from the American occupiers. With Gen. MacArthur's sensitive planning and intelligent governance, Japanese life gradually returned to normal. There may well have been lingering anger, grief or resentment but it was never apparent. Outwardly at least, the people we were able to communicate with in the shops, restaurants, museums and theaters were always cordial, polite and helpful. What they were feeling inside I'll never know. Theirs is an ancient disciplined culture. We visited many of the historical sights and department stores, did a lot of walking, had our first Japanese dinner in a randomly chosen restaurant. Tried Japanese beer (pretty good), bourbon (pretty bad) and *saki* (hot and delicious). And in the evening, as we were wearing down, hopped on the train back to Hiyoshi. These were my first tastes and positive impressions of real Japan and its people.

The following weekend I went to Tokyo alone because I wanted to visit Frank Lloyd Wright's Imperial Hotel unencumbered and at my own pace and leisure. This majestic hotel, a block wide and two blocks deep, was under construction from 1916 to 1922 and opened to great fanfare in 1923. Only a few months later Tokyo was struck by a devastating 7.9 (Richter) earthquake. The hotel was one of the few buildings left standing. But by 1968 this huge building just wore out and would be demolished in favor of a new "Imperial Hotel" on the same site. I was fortunate to be able to spend several hours in this iconic architectural gem, slowly experiencing all the public rooms and gardens, followed by an elegant lunch in the beautifully furnished restaurant. That must have been a sight – this Army Private in uniform dining amid such opulence. It was pretty pricey but I just had to do it. That afternoon I took in a movie at the Ernie Pyle Theater, a huge movie house that showed first run American films.

Although I was learning many new systems and techniques in my classes, it wasn't too difficult and I was doing well. Among the instructors was Master Sgt. Tony Colunga, a career soldier from Fresno, who was a genius with electronics. He had an innovative and curious mind. We seemed to hit it off very well and despite our difference in rank, became good friends. We'd spend many hours talking about the Cold War, Korea, Japan, U.S. politics, education, and so on. Tony had met Yoshiko, a lovely local girl and they fell in love. They lived together in a small, tidy house in Motosumiyoshi. The Army (in fact all branches of the Service) was relentless in trying to discourage servicemen from marrying Japanese or Korean women. But Tony was in love and persisted. He and Yoshi were later married and after his retirement from the Army, moved to Fresno, settled down and raised a family.

Most of my off-duty time was spent exploring Tokyo and Yokohama, usually with others but sometimes alone. There was so much to discover and experience and I immediately took a liking to Japanese food and manners. I would pop in to little hole-in-the-wall sushi shops and try the fish and other miscellaneous (and sometimes mysterious) sea creatures that had been swimming just a few hours earlier. I adapted easily to the local customs, and although no one there knew English, I could manage rudimentary communication. They were always courteous, and pleased and flattered that I was willing to explore their food and culture.

On 5 June 53 my six-week course came to an end. Our tight group and temporary friendships would be splitting up and going our separate ways. As it happened, I turned out to be the top student in the class. I was awarded a letter of commendation from the Commandant and a shiny, beautifully engraved Zippo cigarette lighter. [which I still have] It was useful because I was then a smoker. But was it "luck" or more good timing that on that particular weekend one of the instructors was rotating back to the States and there was now a vacancy that needed to be filled. Colonel Day, the Commandant, summoned me to his office, said some nice things about my achievement and offered me the job. I hesitated for about a nanosecond. I still can't imagine the smile on my face as I floated back to my barracks.

All the others were returned to their units, except the six who had come with me from Camp Drake on another of my lucky days. They were immediately deployed to Korea. After another round of "goodbyes and good lucks" I was left alone in the barracks until later reassignment to a barracks for permanent staff. As I waited there in solitude, I thought of all the seemingly random and meaningless events that strung together to lead me to this moment, altering the course of my life.

After a while I was called to Headquarters to pick up my Orders. The building, the beds, the latrine, everything about my new home was the same as the one I had just left. Except there was a sense of permanence and safety in the air. The anxieties I didn't realize I had just disappeared. This was going to be good. Very good indeed.

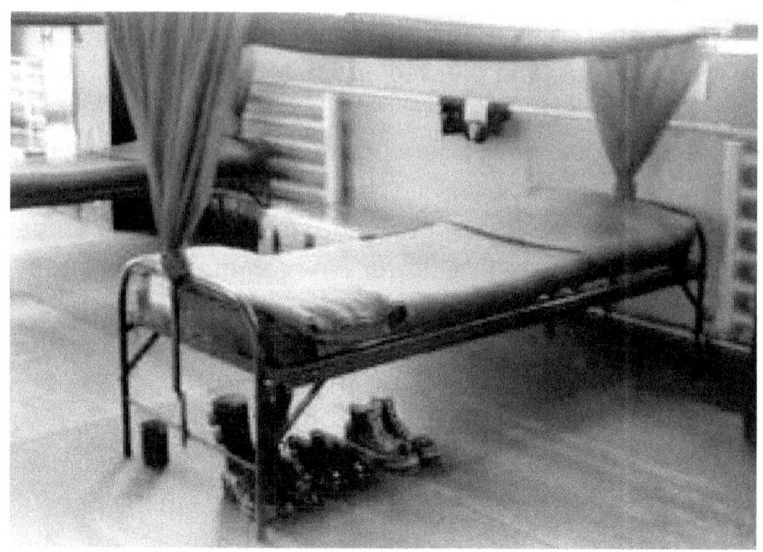
Len's bunk

The new class was not coming in for another week so this week I had no duties. One of the most appreciated perks of being on permanent staff was that I could carry a perpetual pass in my pocket. From noon Saturday till roll call Monday morning I was free to leave camp without requesting a pass. So one of the first things I did was write to my sister Nanie in San Diego asking her to send me some of my civilian clothes. I also went to a department store in Tokyo to buy some shirts and pants. If this place was going to be my home for the next year and a half I might as well feel more like my real self and less defined by the uniform.

JAPAN
Teaching as Permanent Duty

As my first group of students filed into the classroom and took their seats, I waited, a little nervous, in the back of the room. I had never taught anything ever before. But I knew my material and the standard lesson plan for this course was thorough and well organized. My uniform was freshly pressed, my shoes were shiny and I had just gotten a haircut. I walked smartly to the front of the room, introduced myself and made a few announcements. I took roll of about 20 men, ranking from Private to Staff Sergeant and two Second Lieutenants. Some were sent here through the pipeline as I was, while others were from units in Korea, Okinawa and Japan. I went over the rules and outlined what we were going to cover in the next six weeks. I remember as I looked out at them that they all were happy to be here and seemed eager to begin.

And so I began.

The course covered operation, maintenance and interface of the computer and radar systems. Each man had a manual to study after classes. Mornings were spent in the classroom and in the afternoons we were in the yard with hands-on practice on the equipment itself. As the weeks progressed, the material got more detailed and technical, and at the same time I had become completely at ease and confident with my abilities. The class would be tested and graded every week, and by the time they graduated, these men knew and understood, not only the operation, but the electronics involved with these systems and how to repair them. They all tested well, which of course pleased me, so that after a one week break I happily anticipated the arrival of the next class. I came to especially enjoy teaching and demonstrating and explaining, and got to be very good at it. And this is what I did for the next 12 months.

On 9 July 53, during the fifth week of that first class, I was promoted to Private First Class (PFC, with one chevron stripe) at a new pay grade of $103 per month.

JAPAN
Off Duty Life

It was the troops' responsibility in each barracks to keep everything neat and clean. So each soldier in each barracks would chip in a few bucks and a hire a "houseboy." They were usually high school boys eager to learn English and to earn some money. They would come every day and sweep and clean, including the latrines and showers. They would also shine shoes for a few extra yen. Of course, we would make our own beds, crisply tucked according to military standards. Kato, our young helper, was a happy, resourceful boy, smart and endearing. I sometimes wonder what ever became of him. All the men in my barracks were instructors for operation and maintenance of the various components of an anti-aircraft battery. Some of my close friends there included Bernie Goetz, married and a schoolteacher from Ft. Hays, Kansas. He loved baseball and was an avid NY Yankees fan, particularly Mickey Mantle, then at the peak of his career. Bernie and I were teaching the same courses but to different groups of students.

Bernie, Kato and Len

Ed Osborne taught 40 mm and light artillery. He was from Seattle or Portland and loved golf. Somewhere he had obtained a putter and a couple of golf balls and would practice putting along the barracks floor.

Touch football outside one of the barracks buildings

Bill Griffith was from Baltimore and taught heavy artillery (90 mm). He was in a perpetual state of pining for his sweetheart back home and spent his off-duty hours flat on his back on his bed. We called him "prone" but he was easy and good natured about it. In a year and a half I don't think he ever left the camp. Wes Herbst was a tall gangly redhead from Wisconsin who also taught heavy artillery. And there was another fellow, a scholarly type, whose name I just can't recall. He was totally enchanted with Japan and decided to immerse himself as much as he could in Japanese culture and customs, including learning to read, write and speak the language. And he did.

A few weeks after I was all settled in I bought an old bicycle. Bikes in those days were simple and functional -- single speed with coaster brakes, balloon tires, fenders and a basket. Now I was easily able to ride to Motosumiyoshi or Hiyoshi or just around the rural countryside. It was like a refreshing breath of freedom, and exploration became a favorite way to spend an afternoon. Coming upon remote villages and sampling its food and hospitality helped me to gradually appreciate and understand typical Japanese customs and values.

On the other side of the chain link fence surrounding the base were small properties cultivated to produce a variety of vegetables. Children would play there and farmers would tend their crops. I would often go to the fence and call to the kids and they would come scrambling over, bright and playful and eager to make contact. We would have a fun time communicating with physical gestures and a few common words, laughing all the while. I wonder now how they recall those encounters and if those experiences with the American soldiers have in any way affected their lives.

One day I noticed through the fence that a section of crops was being cleared out. A few days later a group of men were laying out the footprint of what appeared to be a house just twenty feet away. I called a couple men over and, yes, they were going to build a farmhouse of about 80-90 square meters (800-900) square feet. Well, of course that was especially exciting to me. I'd be able to watch an indigenous country house being built from the ground up. Every day I observed their methods and compared them with techniques of residential construction in California I was familiar with. The house gradually took form and was completed in about three months. And it was beautiful – simple without affectation, well-proportioned and perfectly suited to its function and place.

But one thing early on in the construction puzzled me. The concrete foundation was poured just as we do here and the foundation wall was about a foot thick and rose about two feet above the ground. Nothing at all unusual. A wood frame wall would be erected on top of the foundation wall. The first part of the wall is called a sill plate. It's a flat horizontal board that lays on top of the foundation. Then the studs (vertical framing) rise up from that. Again, nothing unusual. Until I noticed that the sill plate was not physically attached to the top of the foundation. Although carefully placed, it just laid there. In California the sill plate is firmly bolted to the foundation, and so the entire construction above and the foundation are as one – all stuck together. When the ground moves, as in an earthquake, the whole house tries to move with it. We resist those forces by stiffening the walls and roof so they move as one body with the ground, not distorting and failing. We cope with natural forces by resistance and overcoming them with brute strength.

I asked the workmen about that and isn't the building vulnerable in an earthquake, a frequent occurrence in Japan. My question puzzled them at first, but then they understood and explained that in an earthquake the foundation moves with the ground, but the building above, not being attached to the foundation/ground, is free to slide on the top of the foundation wall with only very minor displacement, usually not more than an inch or two. However, the top of the foundation is wide enough to keep the house from sliding off. This philosophy of accepting nature and "rolling with the punch" and not fighting it with massive reinforcement was something I thought about for several days. I came to suspect this method of construction naturally followed a concept unique to Japanese culture. They find not only beauty in nature but also reverence and respect for natural forces in all its forms. I shared these thoughts with these simple, hardworking men and they happily nodded their approval. And at the same time they were surprised that a Westerner would grasp this.

While browsing through a Popular Mechanics magazine, I came across a piece that looked interesting and challenging. It was a short article on radios but it included a couple of schematic electrical diagrams. After a couple months of teaching operation and repair of the radar and computer systems, I felt competent enough in electronics to tackle a little project of my own. I decided to build a radio. From scratch.

Circuit boards, microchips, transistors and plug-ins had not yet been invented. So starting at the beginning with the latest technology of the time, I bought an aluminum base, about 14" x 9" x 2" high (open underneath), and a small speaker in Motosumiyoshi. All the tools I needed were available in the supply room. And all the parts and components as well, such as wiring, resistors, capacitors and vacuum tubes. Over the next few weeks during off hours I sat at a small table next to my bed arranging and soldering the parts in the underside of the box. The vacuum tubes, the tuning device and the antenna were on the top. I used the tops of toothpaste tubes for the various knobs (on-off, tuning, volume, bass, treble) mounted on the front. When it was finally finished (I hoped), everyone gathered around for the launching. I plugged it into the wall socket (so far so good) and turned it on and paused for a moment (it didn't start smoking). Expectations were high as everyone waited for something to happen. Then I began to turn the tuning dial and turned up the volume. Soon the speaker crackled. Then, abruptly, a lovely Japanese voice singing a current popular song, clearly and without static. Everyone cheered! I stood, smiled and took a most courtly bow.

[A couple years later after I was back in college, I was able to use these electronic skills to build a hi-fi set. Development of stereo in audio was still years in the future and monaural "high-fidelity" was the current state of the art. I bought all the parts at electronic stores and found schematic diagrams of the latest technology for hi-fi components in popular electronics magazines. So I built an amplifier, preamplifier and an am-fm tuner. I also bought a good quality turn-table, a diamond stylus pickup and a decent speaker. Now that I was self-sufficient with my new, one-of-a-kind system, I set out to buy records -- 33 1/3 rpm long play vinyl records. And the first one I bought was an Angel (cheap label, but good quality) recording of Gregorian Chants. What they were singing in Latin didn't matter to me at all; it was the music that was so appealing]

Our Commanding General in charge had a passion for basketball and baseball. He was able to arrange, as only Generals can, to have premier college and professional athletes culled from incoming personnel passing through Camp Drake and be reassigned to his command here. Their official duties were as Military Police (MP) and guards. They had their own barracks and pretty much hung out together. Most of the time many of them would be away competing with other military units and in fact won many championships. The General was happy.

One Friday afternoon he sent a memo to all troops on the base that the baseball team was going to play a game tomorrow in **Nagoya** (in central Japan) and anyone interested in flying down in the morning and returning that night be ready to leave Saturday at 0700 hours. There were about twenty of us that were bussed up to a military airfield near Tokyo. We boarded a C-47 (military designation of the DC-3) outfitted only with long benches along each side. It was a good flight but it was raining when we arrived in Nagoya and the game was canceled. Since the return flight wasn't scheduled until evening, we had the opportunity to explore and experience some of the city. For me, this was even better than the baseball game. Nagoya had been hard hit during the war, but the rebuilding showed very little evidence of the destruction.

After a wet but eventful afternoon and some good Japanese food, we reported back to the air base that evening. The pilot must have had a good afternoon too, because his walk was a bit uncertain and his eyes a little glazed as he stumbled his way to the cockpit. The flight back took about an hour and a half. As we hit the runway, hard, I'm looking out the side window at the ground lights seemingly whizzing by but not slowing down. And we just rolled and rolled. Finally and suddenly, the plane pulled up, just clearing buildings in front of us, and circled around for another pass. The second attempt to land was no better than the first and we banked around and tried it again. Finally, after a bumpy, three-bounce landing, we all gladly clambered out of that airplane. I never saw so many white knuckles.

It was summertime and four of us decided to climb **Mt. Fuji**, its peak visible to us from our camp some 50 miles away. At 10,400 feet, it is Japan's highest and most prominent mountain. Fuji is a revered place and a treasured symbol in Japanese culture. Countless paintings, prints, weavings, screens and so many other forms of art feature this sacred mountain. Its peak is covered with snow in the winter but in summer the snow is melted and people of all ages flock to its base on the broad plain and prepare for the climb. Of course I, like most climbers, bought a wooden hiking stick.

There is a single serpentine trail up the mountain with ten stopping points or stations along the way. At each are light refreshments and places to rest. And for few yen, one can also have his hiking stick stamped with a wood-burning tool noting the station name, number and altitude. Because of the shape of the mountain, the trail starts fairly shallow but becomes gradually steeper the higher one goes. It took about six hours to get to the seventh station and by then it was dark. We ate a little and bedded down for the night at a sleeping hut together with a dozen other climbers. We arose while still dark, had some coffee, and proceeded with our flashlights up the trail. When we reached the summit the eastern sky was ablaze with the promising colors of dawn. Slowly the sun began to rise, spilling its light on the plains far below. The experience was absolutely mesmerizing. It took an hour to walk all around the crater, then the purchase of a small green pennant to tie around the top of my walking stick, and a little hot sake as we planned our descent.

We chose not to take the downward trail but opted instead for a more adven-turous way down. On the other side of the mountain was a two hun-dred foot wide swath of loose lava rock. Because we were wearing our combat boots, we were able step off the rim and land with the other foot six feet out and three feet lower. We continued this way, moving very fast, step over long step sliding through the lava, half way down the mountainside

until we ran out of lava. Then back on the proper trail. The whole descent took about two hours. I still have and cherish my hiking stick.

It was mid-June, 1953. There was an American ham radio operator in Tokyo who, as a generous hobby, offered at no charge calls back to the States. For me, the Tokyo ham operator contacted a partner operator in San Francisco who dialed a long distance call to my home in San Diego. I was able to speak directly to my family for about ten minutes (they paid the long distance charges from San Francisco to San Diego). It worked perfectly. The immediacy of instant voice contact was a wondrous and heartwarming thrill for all of us.

PART 2

One weekend a few of us took a day trip down to **Kamakura**. It's an old coastal city about an hour's train ride south of Hiyoshi. It is a cultural center with numerous temples, shrines and other historical monuments. It had become the political center of Japan in 1192 and continued to rule for over a century. Even after its decline in the 14th century, Kamakura remained the political center of Eastern Japan for some time before losing its position to other cities.

We stopped to have lunch and toured the city and its monuments. But the main reason we went there was to s ee The Great Buddha of Kamakura (Kamakura Daibutsu), a bronze statue of Amida Buddha, which stands on the grounds of Kotokuin Temple.

With a height of 44 feet and weighing 121 tons, it is the second largest bronze Buddha in Japan. The statue was cast in 1252 and was originally located inside a large temple hall. However, the temple buildings were washed away by a tsunami tidal wave in 1498, and since then the Buddha stands in the open air. The Great Buddha is seated in the lotus position with his hands forming the Dhyani Mudra, the gesture of meditation. With a serene expression and a backdrop of wooded hills, the Daibutsu is a truly spectacular sight. Later in the afternoon we found a lovely little restaurant, had a delicious dinner and took the train ride back Hiyoshi.

In late summer I met a fine young Japanese woman named Annie. She was very sweet and had a warm and friendly way about her, and she spoke English quite well. She lived in Moto-sumiyoshi and often after duty hours I would ride my bike to her house to have an authentic Japanese dinner and spend the evening. Sometimes I would wait until after dinner was served in

the mess hall because there were always leftovers that the cooks would happily give me. I'd toss them in my bike's basket and pedal over to Annie's and we'd have an typical American Army meal together. She was bright and thoughtful and we had many intelligent conversations, provocative and challenging. Soon we began taking short trips, mostly to places neither of us had been to before. She was a very good traveling companion, and of course wherever we went, her ability to communicate was far better than mine.

In September Annie and I went for a weekend down the coast to **Atami**. It is south of Yokohama and about an hour and a half train ride from Hiyoshi. We bought box lunches to eat on the train, a common custom. Atami is a small town on the east coast of Japan's Izu Peninsula, and has long been a favored resort for Tokyoites. It rises out of the sea in a slow curve that suddenly steepens into the

imposing hills that overlook the town. Eons ago these hills formed one side of a volcano, the other side lost to the sea. The town is built in the remnants of the crater. With this geological history, there are hot springs all over the area, which, along with its fine views of the sea, makes it the ideal hot springs resort.

We stayed in a lovely *ryokan* with *tatami* mat floors and sliding *shoji* panels that opened out to the spectacular views of the bay.

> [Tatami mats are woven from straw and are usually two meters by one meter and about five cm thick .The edges are bound with a stiff black cloth and the mats are placed tightly against one another wall-to-wall. It is used for flooring in typical un-westernized Japanese homes. (one always re-moves one's shoes when entering a Japanese home) Sleeping on soft mattresses as well as eating and sitting on cushions is also directly on the mats.]

The meals of course were traditional Japanese cuisine served on finely crafted dinnerware. The presentations of the several small courses were simple and elegant, and the careful attention to the color and placing of each item reminded me of the composition and beauty of the *ikebana* (flower arranging). These kinds of observations served to further open me to the qualities and values of this new culture I was so fortunate to be in. I didn't know what half the stuff was that I ate, but I was anxious to try it all, much to Annie's surprise. It was all so delicious with so many textures and flavors. We also indulged in one of the many hot springs, my first time. Pretty darn good. The weather was clear and warm for our two days there and we explored the town from one end to the other.

[Years later when I returned to college, six of us rented a wonderful big house on Indian Rock Road in Berkeley with a breathtaking view across San Francisco Bay clear to the Golden Gate Bridge. Most of us were architecture majors. There were three bedrooms and we paired up for each bedroom Stu Greenfield with Ron Russo and Mack McKamey with me. Stu, Mack and I had all been to Korea or Japan. Mack had loved Japan as much as I did and we decided to make a tatami floor in our room. We bought several 6' x 3' flat straw mats with black edge binding. As Mack was sewing the edges together with thick black thread, I went out and bought scraps of felt undercarpet padding – enough for four layers – and laid them down very carefully. Then we spread the tatami "carpet", which of course fit perfectly. And that was our room for a year]

When the High Holidays came around in the fall, I got three days off to attend services for Rosh Hashana and two days for Yom Kippur. Services were conducted by a Jewish Chaplain and were held in a military facility in Tokyo for the many Jewish servicemen in the area.

I wanted to send something home to my folks so I started to think about what would be useful to them and represent fine Japanese craft. I decided to look for some dinnerware and went to a large department store in Tokyo. There were so many wonderful designs and qualities to choose from that when I found a particularly exquisite set that was so very beautiful, I knew that it would be perfect. The store carefully packed and crated it for me and shipped it off to my mother. Several weeks later when they opened this large shipment they were happily surprised with a 112-piece service for twelve made by Sango. All pieces arrived intact. Mom was overjoyed and so proud. She was a wonderful cook and hosted many delicious and joyous dinners but used this set only for special occasions (and whenever I would come over).

[After my parents died I chose to inherit this set of dishes that provided them so much pleasure. And now I am granted the pleasure of deep connection when I use them on my own special occasions]

Dave Raznick and I were pals as teenagers in Omaha where our parents were very close friends. I learned that he too was stationed in Japan and I tracked him down to the hospital in Tokyo where he was a cook. We got together many times and he often showed me neighborhoods and interesting places that I would otherwise not have known or visited. And, with some of his friends, we'd hit a few bars and clubs. Sometimes I'd eat with him at the hospital. He was a jolly fellow, and with a comedic sense of humor performed frequently on stage. We laughed a lot and had good times together. It was in early July that he rotated back to the States.

I met (I can't remember where) a very nice young Japanese man named Saito and his lovely fiancee Kimiko. They spoke pretty fair English and were anxious to learn more. They were bright and curious about American ways and culture. I frequently went to their home for lunch or dinner and we would have stimulating conversations about a variety of events and ideas. Sometimes they would take me to local shrines, museums and gardens. Then we'd dine at a restaurant or sushi house where I was introduced to unusual and delicious local delicacies. And through them I met other Japanese men and women of this generation. When I left Japan, Saito and Kimiko were thinking about emigrating to Mexico (*Mekishko*, as they called it). We lost touch and I don't know if they ever did move.

Most of my after-work getaways with my buddies were south to Yokohama. About a 15-20 minute train ride took us to the center of town. It seemed like we explored everything, usually ending up in some bar. Beer was the drink of choice but I didn't care much for beer (then). So I tried something else – creme de cacao, a 60-proof liqueur that was sweet and chocolaty and delicious. It was served in a small glass and I could sip it slowly and make it last while they were guzzling several beers. And this became my drink of choice whenever we would go carousing in Yokohama or Tokyo.

Sometimes we'd get hungry and stop off at our favorite little café for yakusoba, which I came to love. Yakusoba is a stir-fried noodle dish in which is mixed small pieces of pork and shrimp, special sauce, carrots, onion, bell pepper, cabbage, mushrooms, and pickled ginger and seaweed for garnish.

[For years after returning to San Diego, I could not find yakusoba served in any of the local Japanese restaurants, but in recent years it has become popular and available]

Early one spring morning the whole AAA Battery loaded up all the equipment, radar/fire control, 90 mm anti-aircraft artillery and assorted munitions, and drove out to a coastal region for live practice. It was cold and it was rainy when we got there and set up our equipment. The targets were expendable radio-controlled drone aircrafts. They made about a couple dozen passes over the course of the day but we didn't hit a damn thing.

On 15 January 54 I was promoted to Corporal (two stripes) that included a raise to $128 per month.

I wanted very much to visit **Kyoto**, the ancient cultural center of all Japan. It is revered by the Japanese for its centuries-old temples, shrines, parks and gardens. Although ravaged by wars, fires, and earthquakes during its eleven centuries as the imperial capital, Kyoto was spared from the firebombing of World War 2. With its 2,000 Buddhist temples and Shinto shrines, as well as palaces, gardens and architecture intact, it is one of the best preserved cities in Japan.

Kyoto became the seat of Japan's imperial court in 794 and remained Japan's capital until the transfer of the government to Edo (Tokyo) in 1868.

On 28 Dec 53 I got a one-week leave and Annie and I took the train south through the fertile, green countryside of Honshu. She had never been to Kyoto before and was excited to be going. After several hours we stopped at Osaka on the coast and then proceeded inland to Kyoto. It was raining when we arrived and when we left the station we quickly found a nice small hotel where we were able to dry out and make some plans. A small shop nearby had maps and guide books and I bought all I could carry. Kyoto is renowned for its abundance of delicious Japanese foods and cuisine. So after a leisurely and simple lunch, and with new umbrellas, we set out to discover Kyoto.

The Heian-jingu Shrine was built in 1895 to commemorate the 1,100th anniversary of the capital being moved to Kyoto. Its entrance is through a bright orange, 24 meter high torii gate. This Shinto Shrine is also renowned for its beautiful gardens with traditional Japanese landscaping. In addition to the immense fore-court, the Shrine itself is surrounded by 33,000 square meters of traditional 'Meiji-era' style Japanese gardens. One of the popular features of
the Heian gardens is sakura, or cherry-blossom viewing (hanami) n spring. Alas, we were just too early.

Ryoan-ji Temple in Kyoto is famous for its Zen garden, one of the most notable examples of the "dry-landscape" style. Some say Ryoan-ji Temple garden is the quintessence of Zen art, and perhaps the single greatest masterpiece of Japanese culture. Surrounded by low walls, an austere arrangement of fifteen rocks sits on a bed of raked white gravel. That's it --- no trees, no hills, no ponds, no trickling water. Nothing you could describe as romantic, distracting or pretty. But its minimalism inspires something else – contemplation, introspection, and deliberation on the transience of our own humanity.

No one knows who laid out this simple garden, or precisely when, but it is today as it was yesterday, and tomorrow it will be as it is today. Behind the simple temple that overlooks the rock garden is a stone washbasin called *Tsukubai,* said to have been contributed by Tokugawa Mitsukuni in the 17th century. It bears a simple but profound four-character inscription: "I learn only to be contented."

Kinkaku-ji (The Golden Pavilion) is set in a magnificent Japanese strolling garden. The pond in front of it is called Kyoko-chi (Mirror Pond). There are many islands and stones on the pond that represent the Buddhist creation story.

The 1st floor is in the ancient palace style. Both the 2nd and 3rd floors are in different styles and are covered with gold-leaf on Japanese lacquer. The roof is thatched with shingles. There had been a fire in 1950 that completely destroyed the building. The reconstruction was almost finished with just the shingles to be installed. As a fund-raiser, they were "selling" shingles and we bought a couple shingles upon which they painted our names.

Ginkaku-ji (The Silver Pavilion) was built in 1474 by the shogun Ashikaga Yoshimasa, who sought to emulate the Golden Pavilion Kinkakuji Temple commissioned by his grandfather Ashikaga Yoshimitsu.

During the O-nin War in the mid-15th century, construction was halted. Despite Yoshimasa's intention to cover the structure with a distinctive silver foil overlay, this work was delayed for so long that the plans were never realized before Yoshimasa's death. The present appearance of the structure is understood to be the same as when Yoshimasa himself last saw it. This "unfinished" appearance illustrates one of the aspects of "wabi-sabi" quality.

Wabi-sabi represents a comprehensive Japanese world view or aesthetic centered on the acceptance of transience. The aesthetic is sometimes described as one of beauty that is "imperfect, impermanent, and incomplete" Characteristics of the wabi-sabi aesthetic include asymmetry, asperity, simplicity, modesty, intimacy, and suggest a natural process.

Wabi-sabi is thought to be the most conspicuous and characteristic feature of what we think of as traditional Japanese beauty, and is said to occupy roughly the same position in the Japanese pantheon of aesthetic values as do the Greek ideals of beauty and perfection in the West. If an object or expression can bring about, within us, a sense of serene melancholy and a spiritual longing, then that object could be said to be "wabi-sabi."

The Katsura Imperial Villa (Katsura Rikyu) is one of the finest examples of purely Japanese architecture and garden design and is one of the nation's finest architectural treasures. The villa and garden in their present form were completed in 1645 as the residence for the Katsura Family, members of Japan's Imperial Family.

The gardens of the Katsura Imperial Villa are a masterpiece of Japanese gardening, and the buildings are even more important, one of the greatest achievements of Japanese architecture. The palace includes a shoin (building), tea houses, and a strolling garden. It provides an invaluable window into the villas of princes of the Edo period.

Annie and I visited so many beautiful shrines and temples and lush gardens and ponds. The weather for the most part was overcast and cold. Three days were of intermittent rain, but two days were really sunny and pleasant. On New Year's Eve it snowed and the next day, needless to say, was just glorious. The less than perfect weather did not at all deter us from our eager and rewarding explorations, and we managed just fine. This was a wonderful and profoundly enlightening trip.

Back to teaching again. Although the courses were pretty routine by now, each new batch of students provided me enough stimulus to enthusiastically begin again. That they did very well on the exams was indicative of my effectiveness, and that was very gratifying. In mid-January it started snowing, the first snowfall of the year in the Tokyo-Yokohama area. After a couple days there was a foot of snow on the ground. We would throw snowballs at each other, but soon that wore thin because it was warmer and drier inside.

It was late in January that a new Army directive came down concerning seasonal occupations permitting early separation of up to three months prior to scheduled discharge date. This would allow me to be separated early in order to begin the fall semester at Cal. I could be getting out about the first of September instead of October 21, and would probably leave Japan about August 1 instead of mid-September. From an earlier inquiry, I had already received verification from Cal that I can be readmitted when separated from the Army, but I needed to wait until late April to file an official application for readmission. And I would have the benefits of the G.I. Bill. Then I had another idea.

My "3-month early date" was 21 July 1954. So I applied to San Diego State College for their Second Summer Session beginning August 9 and lasting only three weeks. A few weeks later I received official notice of admission and immediately filed the necessary paperwork for early discharge from the Army. On 3 May 54 I was approved for release from active duty on 1 August 1954. My new sailing date was 15 June 54.

During one of my solo visits to Tokyo I stumbled onto a wonderful discovery in the Shinjuku District in the southern part of the city. I was walking down a busy noisy street one evening when I heard some lovely classical music wafting out of an otherwise ordinary doorway, and when I entered discovered I was in a small coffee house. I had never seen a coffee place like this. The menu included coffees from all over the world as well as complicated blends of as many as six or seven or eight varieties. The room was softly lit and simply furnished with small tables. People generally sat silently or spoke in hushed tones so as not to disturb others' enjoyment of the music. And it was the music that was so appealing, played on state-of-the-art high fidelity equipment. And with the wonderful aromas and delicious coffees it was like stepping into another world. I remember so vividly that on that first night I sat alone at one of those small tables sipping my coffee and listening, rapt, to Brahms' Violin Concerto. [And even now, whenever I hear that stunningly beautiful piece, I am instantly transported back, for a few moments, to that charming little coffee oasis]

I would return there frequently and the staff got to know me, as I was their only American customer. They would recommend different coffee blends for me to try and would also ask if there was something in particular I would like to hear. The Japanese have a hard time pronouncing Ls and Vs, so I was known as **Reni Bai-tsa-ru** and affectionately called **Reni-san**. Over the next few months I spent many tranquil hours in my new favorite place.

And this is where I met Michiko.

She was a lovely twenty year old college student who popped in early one evening for coffee and music and sat at a nearby table, intending to do some homework. We got to talking (her English was very good) and found that we had many interests in common. After about an hour, as she needed to study and I needed to return to camp, we agreed to meet here a few days later. We did, and spent several swift-seeming hours surrounded by beautiful music and talking about so many things. It soon became clear that we were attracted to each other. And so we began dating on a regular basis. She lived in Tokyo with her family so we would always meet somewhere else that was mutually convenient. We went on many outings and picnics and took short day trips to nearby places where I had never been. We visited lovely parks and art galleries, saw movies, Kabuki theatre and Noh plays, and often returned to "our" coffee shop. And over time we grew very close to falling in love.

I had been a "short timer" for about a month when, during the first week of June 1954, I received my shipping orders back to the States. I had a few days left for my last class and it was with a certain amount of joy and regret that I prepared to pack up and go home. The rounds of good-byes with my fellow soldiers were bittersweet, for we all knew we'd likely never see one another again. And it was so terribly difficult and far too poignant as I bade that tearful farewell to Michiko. On that last night in my barracks I lay sleepless on my bunk bed for hours recalling the many experiences and discoveries of the past fourteen months, as if not wanting to let them go. I had been profoundly affected by this ancient, but new to me, culture in ways I was yet to realize.

ON THE PACIFIC AGAIN
The Journey Home

On June 14th another rotating soldier and I were driven early in the morning to Camp Drake to reverse the process I had experienced some fourteen months earlier. It took only a few hours and the next morning I was on a train with a large group of other men heading to dockside in Yokohama. We boarded the troop transport USNS Gen. J.C. Breckinridge and were assigned quarters. And of course the first thing I did after settling in was to seek out the chaplain and volunteer to work on the ship's newspaper. He was glad to have me. The relief from other duties was just as I had hoped, just like on the earlier trip. Again, there were about 3,000 troops on board, now mostly as corporals, and a few sergeants and officers. Most of the soldiers and Marines had served their time in Korea and their relief to be on this ship was almost palpable.

As the ship cast its lines and we began to ease away from the dock, I, along with many others, lined the rail as if, in a way, to say goodbye. Soon we were leaving the harbor and moving slowly out into the open sea. I lingered on deck for a long while and watched Japan recede slowly away. As much as I was anxious to return home and get back to my family and school, I was so deeply grateful for my good fortune to have been here for such a fruitful and unforgettable time. And I also realized that I had profoundly grown and changed.

Then my thoughts drifted to Michiko, and as I reflected on our tender friendship, wondered what would become of her as she moved on with her life. And if she too would remember our brief and gentle interlude.

The two-week journey eastward to San Francisco was largely uneventful. The men all had their assigned duties and spent their leisure time reading or playing cards or shooting craps. And a lot of money changed hands on that ship. The mood on board was very upbeat, so much different from the uncertainty and anxiety on our way to Korea. Many were looking forward to civilian life, many to reuniting with their wives and children. After we 'reporters' would get the newspaper out each day we'd swap "war stories", drink coffee and wait for the next meal. And read.

From the ship's library I checked out Pearl Buck's *The Hidden Flower,* a touching love story set in Japan. But more importantly it reminded me of how my own life, indeed my maturing inner eye, was expanded by discovering Japanese culture's profound respect for nature and deep reverence for beauty. In fact a couple memorable lines have stayed with me and guided me ever since, not only in my approach to architecture, art and design, but most significantly the way I've chosen to live my life.

"These were men who understood beauty. They were connoisseurs, comprehending that form without spirit is void, and this comprehension led them from one step to another in pursuit of beauty for spirit's sake, man and nature in complete unity. Thus they believed that the principles of beauty must permeate every detail and article in life, architecture, ceramics, decoration. To achieve simplicity was the ultimate of sophistication. The fully matured mind reaches simplicity as its final development."

I also read James Michener's just-published *Sayonara,* which centered on the ill-fated romance of an American officer and a Japanese woman. The poignant similarities to my romance with Michiko were unmistakable. And then another similar-themed Michener book, *The Bridges at Toko-Ri,* published a year earlier. So for me, the journey back was not only filled with optimism and anticipation, but was also a time for introspection and contemplation.

[Years later, upon my first experience with the exquisite music and tragic love story of Puccini's *Madama Butterfly,* I was thrust back in time and place, and sadly wept. *Butterfly* is still my favorite opera, where I still shed heartfelt tears]

What a glorious sight it was to be gliding under the Golden Gate Bridge on the clear, sunny afternoon of June 30, 1954. I had been across this bridge many times but this was different. I was coming back to my home. This connection was inescapable and deeply felt, for as much as I enjoyed Japan and cherished my experiences, I was so very happy to be back.

Actual photo of USNS J.C. Breckinridge
approaching San Francisco
on 30 June 1954

I AM ON IT AT THIS MOMENT !!!

We filled the deck of the Breckinridge as we slowly eased against the dock at Ft. Mason. To our astonishment the dock was packed with people cheering and waving small flags. A military band played rousing marches and everyone on shore was excited and jubilant. The gangplanks were lowered and we slowly disembarked, each man carrying his bulging duffel bag. Waiting families embraced their long gone loved ones and after a while we were ordered to load up into waiting busses which would transport us for two hours down the coast to Ft. Ord. The same place where this adventure all started for me some 21 months earlier.

As I was going through processing with a myriad of paperwork, one of the clerks there was Myron Shelley, an old friend of mine from San Diego. He was as surprised to see me as I was to see him. He was drafted as I was but managed to get stationed there at Ft. Ord. We planned to get together later. I had a lot of accrued leave and as soon as I was settled into my new quarters (barracks) I requested and was granted a 3-day pass.

I took a Greyhound Bus to the downtown San Diego bus station where my folks were waiting. What a wonderful reunion we all had as I began to tell them well into the night of some of my experiences. It was all too brief, as I had to return to Ft. Ord in two days.

My father had just bought a new '54 Plymouth and I had prearranged with him to buy his "old car." So a couple days later, with a new batch of civilian clothes, I happily headed north in my light blue 1948 Plymouth sedan.

Ft. Ord is a huge army base about half way between Santa Cruz and Monterey with several entrance gates from the main highway (US 101). I entered the main gate and was directed to a parking lot near my assigned barracks. I got settled in and early the next morning reported to the first formation of the day. After roll call everyone went to breakfast. After breakfast another formation was called (<u>but without roll call</u>) and duty assignments were made – mostly K.P. By the end of the day I was exhausted and smelly. The final roll call formation was after dinner. And the next day was the same. That evening I got together with Myron at the NCO (non-commissioned officers) Club. He told me that about a half mile south was the Officers' section and that their gate was never manned.

It was still early July and my discharge date was not until August 1. The prospect of a month of K.P. was too odious for me to contemplate. I had to do something.

So the next morning I was at the first roll call formation, had breakfast and skipped the second formation (no roll call). Instead, I stuck a bathing suit in my pocket, got in my car and drove to the Officers' section. It was true – no one was at the gate and I drove right out onto the highway 101. About a half hour later I was in Carmel, just south of Monterey. I spent the whole day at the beautiful beach, walked all over this charming town and got to know the village extremely well. I finally headed back to Ft. Ord about 4:30, had dinner and made the final formation and roll call. And I followed this routine daily for the next three and a half weeks. No one, except Myron, was ever the wiser.

As scheduled, I was discharged on August 1, 1954. I said goodbye to Myron and as I drove leisurely down the coast, I couldn't help but reflect back on the last 21 months of this journey. At the same time I was thinking forward about returning to Cal and the six weeks leading up to that. I am supposed to start a three-week Summer Session at San Diego State on August 9. But by the time I got to San Diego that evening I had rolled around in my head the odds of the Army checking to see if I was indeed enrolled. I finally presumed that they had more important matters to be concerned with, and decided to chance it. I had presumed correctly -- the Army never checked. I did not enroll at San Diego State but instead looked for a short term drafting job. I found one immediately with Fred Liebhardt, a young and very talented architect. His office was in a funky old weathered wood cottage overlooking the Cove in La Jolla. He had spent a year at Wright's Taliesin West near Phoenix. His sensitivity to Japanese culture and design resonated so well with my own recent experiences that we became especially good friends, although I worked for him for just six weeks. I was excited and anxious to get back to school and continue my studies for the next year and a half. In mid-September I packed all my stuff into the Plymouth, kissed everyone goodbye and drove up to Berkeley, a much different man than when I had left.

LEN VEITZER
January 2015

THE GUTBUCKET BLUES AND WAY TOO MUCH BOOZE

It was a calm and balmy Saturday evening in early October. Unseasonably so, almost warm. Not with the usual chilled autumn breeze coming off the bay. Red and orange and yellow leaves were painting a colorful carpet along the streets in the wooded neighborhoods of North Berkeley. I was 25 and just finishing my architectural studies at the University.

And I was at a party with four pals at someone's home. It was a pretty good party but around nine o'clock we all left and piled into George's car. He was a little older and owned the very popular North Gate Coffee shop on Euclid Avenue. George was going to take us to another party at the home of a friend of his high up in the Berkeley hills. The narrow street was crowded with parked cars but we were able to find a spot a half block away and yet could still hear the joyous music and the hubbub of happy sounds. We walked through the lighted entry garden and joined dozens of revelers in this beautiful contemporary house designed by Roger Lee, a noted Bay Area architect. We were immediately greeted by our host, Scott Newhall, the genial pioneering editor of the San Francisco Chronicle. He giddily poured whatever spirits we wanted but he had no mixers, like coke, soda, ginger ale, seven-up, juice or even water. But he did have champagne, lots of champagne, and that's what he used no matter what was in our glasses. It took a little getting used to, but that didn't take long.

The party was humming. It was crowded, men and women of all ages happily tinkling glasses and engaging in animated conversations. Some were dancing. There was no particular occasion for this party, just a typically spontaneous Newhall gathering. And central to all this was a jamming pickup band. Two fellas brought their cornet and clarinet and were gleefully blowing away. The great grinning piano player pounded on the keys. Another beat away on makeshift drums consisting of cardboard boxes and pots and pans. But the deep bass linear beat was supplied by an old black guy joyfully strumming away on the gutbucket. I was mesmerized, just standing there and watching him. He had noticed, and at the break he asked me if I'd like to try it. Being pretty well lubricated with a couple more scotch and champagne cocktails I said 'sure!' And he proceeded to show me how to make a gutbucket sing.

A gutbucket is fashioned from a washtub turned upside down, and a hole, about 1/4" diameter, is drilled through the bottom. A short length of clothesline rope is knotted at one end and threaded through the hole from below with the knot fitting tightly against the hole. The rope's open end is then tied around the top of a broomstick. The player stands with one foot on the edge of the upside down tub to keep it in place while the broomstick is thrust against the rim of the tub. By skillfully pulling gently on the broomstick and varying the tension on the rope while strumming it, a deep bass-like thump of any note can be produced by the tub.

When the music resumed and with the amused permission of the other musicians, I joined the piece and began strumming away. And to my astonished amazement, as well as to everyone else's, I picked up the rhythm instantly and quickly found the right notes. I plunked away for three or four numbers, grinning gleefully and having the time of my life. When I stepped down I was awarded a nice round of applause.

By now it was getting late but one of the guests invited us to his house on Oxford Street for a nightcap and we left the party about midnight. I was, as they say, three sheets to the wind, and don't remember much except that it seemed we were there at his house a long time, repeatedly toasting each other. I ultimately fell into a haze.

But when it had suddenly become eerily quiet I surfaced from my drunken stupor, feeling the host's hand on my thigh. Whoa! Everyone was gone and we were alone there on the couch. I sprang to my feet and bolted down the stairs and sprinted out the front door. As I got to the sidewalk I could see the tail lights of the car disappearing down the street. My frenzied shouts were ingloriously lost in the still night air.

It was two o'clock in the morning and I was about a mile from home. So I began walking south on Oxford the few blocks to Hearst and past the formal west entrance to the campus, and then to Bancroft. I must have been a staggering sight, lurching as best I could. I had to take particular care crossing all the streets and fortunately there was no traffic. I continued on to Dwight and hurriedly turned west across Oxford. Two blocks later was Shattuck Avenue, Berkeley's main north-south street, and there was a good deal of traffic. I weavingly waited for a green light and hastily crossed. Then the half block to this stately old Victorian that I called home.

I had half the lower floor and with a great sigh of relief, I went straight to the bedroom, ripped off my clothes and flopped onto the bed. I think I must have bounced because as soon as I laid myself out I was up again with the urgency of a desperately wretched stomach. I staggered into the bathroom and thrust my head into the toilet and retched it all out, over and over again. Finally, totally exhausted, my belly aching and with the sourest taste my mouth had ever known, I gave up. I folded and fell asleep, there in the dark, onto the cold tile of the bathroom floor.

I must have slept there on the floor for the better part of an hour and when I awoke crawled groggily back to the bedroom. My stomach had begun to settle down but I had a bodacious headache. I was still one sorry-looking sick puppy! I crumpled onto the bed and thankfully fell quickly asleep.

It must have been around nine o'clock when I was awakened by a tapping on the window next to my bed. It hurt to open my eyes but when I did, there was Adrienne, my upstairs neighbor, needing to borrow a couple eggs. I motioned for her to come in the front door which I had been too dazed to lock when I came home.

When she came into the bedroom and stood so tall and imperially next to the bed with me lying there buck nekkid, she smiled wickedly for the longest while but then, chuckling, pulled a sheet over me. But Adrienne was a good soul and to my everlasting gratitude, could sympathize with my distress. With gentle amusement she threw some clothes at me, put up a pot of coffee, made some toast and tenderly nursed me for a couple hours until I could again feel functional. Of course she was curious about what had brought me to this very sorry state so I told her, unabashedly and in great detail, about my night's adventures and misadventures.

That evening I finally began to feel close to normal and thought about the last 24 hours and what, if anything, I could take from it. For one thing, my unmusical me managed to learn and play passably well the gutbucket. So what! Well, it felt good to have accomplished something so totally unexpected.

But more importantly I learned the value of moderation. Not just with alcohol but in other activities that would affect most aspects of my life. While still being curious and adventurous in seeking a wide variety of experiences, I wisely grew to be a little more prudent and a little less impulsive about making extreme choices.

But alas, I'm still waiting for an invitation for a gutbucket encore.

LEN VEITZER
July 2014

KENYA, PROFOUNDLY

In 1984 my wife Nadene and I spotted a small notice in the local newspaper about a photo safari to Africa, more precisely Kenya. It was being organized by the San Diego Zoo and would ultimately include eighteen participants. Bob Harms, a San Diego resident, owned and operated *Harmsafari*, a safari tour company in Nairobi, Kenya and he would be organizing the 23-day tour during the summer. Joan Embery and her husband Duane Pillsbury are to be the tour coordinators. Travel arrangements were most capably arranged by Louise and Bernard Streiff at Rancho San Diego Travel.

We flew from San Diego to JFK in New York and then on a PanAm 747 to Africa. After a long and tedious flight we landed in Lagos, Nigeria for refueling. Bur then the crew could not get the door to close properly and discovered it was broken, so they had to have a replacement door delivered. We all disembarked and waited in the passenger lounge with armed soldiers watching our every move. We were stuck on the ground for five hours until finally summoned back to the plane. The new door held fast during the six hour trip to Nairobi and although weary, we were all happy and relieved to finally get there. It had been a 24 hour trip. From the airport we were whisked to the venerable Norfolk Hotel, a storied relic from Kenya's colonial days.

A couple days later we motored north by coach toward the Lakes. Particularly fascinating was the endless variety of birds at Lake Naivasha and the more than a million pink flamingos crowding the shores of Lake Nakuru. And also the nighttime viewing from the Treetops Lodge, which is raised high on stilts overlooking an illuminated watering hole and salt lick.

We then motored to the Mt. Kenya Safari Club at the foot of Mt. Kenya to spend a couple days in this remnant of the British Colonialism. Its influence was obvious everywhere from the furnishings, the manners and the exquisite tableware in the dining room. Women were required to wear skirts or dresses to dinner and men to wear coat and tie. The grounds were carefully and beautifully maintained as several peacocks roamed around, showing off as peacocks are wont to do.

We continued motoring north to the Samburu Reserve and the Lodge just in time for high tea on the verandah overlooking the Uoso

91

Nyiro River, teeming with enormous crocodiles. The game runs the next day were wondrous and spectacular. Then to the Lewa Downs Ranch for three days, a private 40,000 acre reserve with an abundance of wildlife and accommodations in very comfortable tents.

We clambered aboard three twin-engine Cessnas and flew from the Lewa Downs Ranch south to the dirt landing strip at Amboseli and settled into private huts right there in the shadow of Mt. Kilimanjaro, just across the border in Tanzania. Then after a couple days of large herds of elephant runs, finally back to Nairobi.

We had first class accommodations throughout the journey, together with carefully prepared and delicious gourmet cuisine. The entire safari was exceptionally well organized and efficiently managed. Our primary guide was British with a dozen years experience and our native guides seemed to have an uncanny sense of where to find the game. We were able to observe elephants, zebras, rhinos, gazelles, stampeding wildebeests fording a river, lions, cheetahs, hyenas, leopards, hippos, giraffes, jackals, wild dogs, dik diks, oryx, cape buffalos, baboons, impalas, kudus and so many smaller animals. And birds. Birds of every imaginable type. We witnessed nature's way with the chasing, the killing and then the devouring, followed by the furious, shrieking vultures doing their cleanup work. All this had its own kind of beauty that was in fact particularly sobering. The whole experience for me was beyond expectations.

But the highlight for me, and the most memorable, was the Masai Mara. It is a game reserve that covers 700 square miles in the southwest of Kenya, adjoining the Serengeti National Park in Tanzania. The countryside in the Mara is some of the most beautiful in Kenya, with rolling grassland plains and hills, dense thickets of scrub, acacia woodland, river forest and swamps. And we were to spend three days there.

At the Norfolk Hotel we were loaded into four open-topped Nissan range vehicles and driven for two hours to the Mara. When we arrived at the campsite everything had been prepared for our stay. A kitchen truck had preceded us and under a large tent two tables with white linen tablecloths and elegant tableware awaited us. It was already late in the afternoon so we all gathered around a campfire for a cordial cocktail hour. Then to the delicious dinner, served with style and grace and imported exceptional wines. By now night had fallen and we all returned to the campfire for shots of fresh Kenyan coffee.

This was a tented camp. Spread about were two-person tents, each with a w.c. and a sink. Open-air showers with wraparound curtains were set up under a tree. After a long and eventful day we all settled in for the night anxiously anticipating our first run in the morning. Animals are up at dawn and out hunting. Then most would find shelter and sleep during the very hot day and return to the hunt in late afternoon. So we were all up by 5 o'clock and after breakfast loaded into our four vehicles. On this morning we drove to the edge of a low hill overlooking a vast, limitless plain glistening in the early morning light. The sky was bright, the air was crisp and it was eerily quiet. Our vehicle happened to stop in front of the others on the edge of the hill. I quickly stood up and poked my head through the open top, camera at the ready. And I was frozen with awe.

There was nobody in front or to the side of me. I could see no one, and I began to feel completely alone. I had never seen such a big sky. It stretched beyond my peripheral vision and overwhelmed my sense of perspective. But the endless vastness of the plain below was the most affecting. I had brought a zoo mentality with me to Kenya: The giraffes are over here. The elephants are over there. The lions, the zebras and the rhinos are all in their separate enclosures.

But here, in this typical African environment, they are all together in one great panorama, roaming, foraging and intermingling, and except for the big cats and other predators off by themselves, not threatening or isolated. It was mesmerizing.

And then the most profound realization enveloped me. I could have been standing here a hundred years ago, or five hundred, or a thousand and this is exactly what I would see. The very same thing. I've been to Yosemite and the Grand Canyon and walked around the top of Mt. Fuji. I've marveled at their grandeur and beauty, but what I have gazed upon this day is fundamentally different. It is teeming with life. It always has. And here I stand now, in my own blink of a moment in time, connecting with this seemingly infinite world.

LEN VEITZER
May 2018

DISCOVERING FRANCE

In the late summer of 1989, after two years of difficult negotiations, my divorce was finally approaching resolution. My three year architectural partnership with Jerry Shonkwiler had sadly folded a year earlier during an economic downturn when we just ran out of work. All my five children were grown, had graduated from their various colleges and were launched into their adult lives. I was used to taking on all kinds of responsibilities as a matter of course without really thinking much about it. But now I began to realize that for the first time in my adult life I was no longer responsible for anyone or anything. No wife, no dependent children, no clients, no business or employees. No one. I could do whatever I wanted and go wherever I pleased. Indeed, a very heady feeling, ripe with opportunities and optimism.

I was ready and eager for some changes, and so I began to think about serious traveling, maybe even moving. All my children lived elsewhere, and except for friends, there was nothing very important keeping me in San Diego. And despite approaching my 60th birthday in a few months, I was healthy, energetic and resilient. I was open now to anything, and with what could be a major change of life for me, I began to explore the possibilities of where and when to go.

Europe had always been appealing to me, and although I had traveled there many times to several countries, there was still much to discover. Having lived most of my life relishing the temperate climate of San Diego, I wanted something similarly agreeable in Europe. That precluded the northern countries and so I quickly focused on the Mediterranean coast. I had visited and loved Greece. And I very much enjoyed Italy the several times I journeyed there. Spain was tempting, but not enough so. This led me to think about France, specifically the South, and the more I rolled around the idea, the more compelling it became. Three of my children had been to Provence during their high school study-abroad summers and found it such a lovely and interesting place. So that was one area I knew something about. But the South of France stretches from Italy to Spain along the northern shore of the Mediterranean and so, for me, there were so many possible destinations about which I knew nothing.

I began my research by buying a passel of those superb Michelin maps of the entire southern half of France. I studied them thoroughly, tracing all the highways, roads and byways and identifying the cities, towns and villages. I got a pretty good lay of the land. Then I purchased travel guides, picture books and anything else I could find on the South of France. All in all, dozens of books, including several by MFK Fisher, the eminent foodie and writer about Aix-en-Provence, and Peter Mayle, who lived and wrote about "A Year in Provence." These were all informative and helpful references describing the cities and towns I observed on the maps. And with each day of learning about the South of France my excitement and anticipation grew until ….. a plan began to develop.

> Explore the region first to discover that exceptional
> place that would be my next home.
> Book flights from San Diego to Nice in mid-October
> 1989, returning three weeks later.
> Pre-lease a car for three weeks from Renault, to be
> picked up in Nice.
> Sign up for a four week crash course in French at
> the Language School on India Street.
> Shop for travel items I would need.
> And change a few dollars into francs.

And so I began. Through Louise at Rancho San Diego Travel Agency I booked a round trip on TWA San Diego to JFK through St. Louis, then Air France to Paris, and return three weeks later. From Paris I will travel to Nice by TGV, the bullet train, ticket bought separately. At the end of my stay I will buy a one-way flight from Nice to Paris to pick up my return Air France flight to JFK. Then, when in New York, I will spend a couple days visiting Eli and Pauline, who were living on West 81st Street.

I learned of a terrific auto leasing plan developed by Renault for periods of three weeks to six months. It must be contracted in the U.S. and is far less costly than any other leasing arrangement in Europe. The way the plan worked is that Renault would sell me a brand new car of my choosing (complete with insurance, 24-hour assistance, etc.) from a wide range of Renault autos, and agree to buy it back from me for a pre-determined price at the end of the pre-arranged period (in my case three weeks). The savings are from not having to pay the 19% VAT (value added tax), which car rental agencies must charge. So I selected the Renault 5SL, 4-speed manual, 2-door, white with blue interior, unlimited mileage. Total cost $659.

I took the French class and found it helpful for vocabulary and basic terms. However, there was not enough time to develop conversational skill, as I found out later. But it was a decent start. And I bought $50 worth of French francs (300F) to have in my pocket when I got there. The exchange rate was approximately six francs to the dollar.

On the day before departure I packed a couple bags, got all my papers in order, and together with my trusty brown shoulder bag was ready to go on this wonderful new adventure. I was neither nervous nor apprehensive. I was excited and optimistic and couldn't wait to get going.

In recent years I had come to believe that nothing in our existence is already fated; that is, occurrences and experiences are not happenings that are meant to be. Rather, and except for purposely laid plans to do this or that, our lives and so many meaningful events we experience are affected by the consequences of chance and random intersections. And so, one must get out into the world and sample the maelstrom of experiences that can truly enrich one's life. Of course, there are always some risks, but with thoughtful care and good common sense they can be minimized and managed. And the rewards are limitless. With all this in mind, I was brimming with anticipation and so very anxious to begin.

It was early Tuesday morning, October 17th when Carole took me to Lindbergh Field in San Diego. We lingered at the curb, with very tender goodbyes and with much left unsaid. I hustled inside, went through security and boarded the TWA flight to St. Louis at 6:40 with both carry-ons. I was afraid that if checked, I'd have to wait too long to pick up the luggage with only two hours to catch my Air France connection in New York at 7:00 p.m. local.

At first, the plane's engines wouldn't start, then the fog rolled in, and it was 8:20 when we finally took off. Sausage and eggs for breakfast were pretty good. We missed our first approach in St. Louis but finally landed at 1:20 local. Left for New York an hour later and was served a good seafood lunch which I had requested. There was heavy air traffic at JFK, it was raining and planes were stacked up in landing patterns. Finally arrived at 6:00 p.m. (local time). I found a baggage cart and walked briskly, in and out of the rain, to Air France in the West International Terminal. Checked in at 6:40, boarded and found my seat on the aisle. "Whew!" I thought, "I just knew I could make it." As I settled in, I found Carole's tender and touching note in my green bag. I was flooded with so many conflicting emotions.

Then at 7:30 an announcement stated that a "passenger was missing" belonging to a baggage already stowed. They had to "disembark" all luggage to find the bag. They did, and we finally pulled away from the gate at 7:50, but because of the heavy traffic had to wait another half hour to lift off. So here I am, on Air France Flight #70, a luxurious 747, launching what I hope to be an exceptional discovery. And as an appropriate introduction to well known French standards, an excellent dinner was served, together with a fine vin blanc. I went to sleep about 11:00. The flight was bumpy and it was a fitful sleep.

As we raced toward the sun rising over the horizon of the eastern Atlantic, a fine breakfast of poached eggs, croissant, fruit and coffee was served. It was 8:30 when we landed at CDG (Charles de Gaulle). I breezed through customs and boarded the Air France shuttle. It took an hour through heavy traffic but I was glued to the window, experiencing this new place like an eager wide eyed child. Paris is clear, sunny and brisk (50s F). Near the breathtaking Arc de Triomphe

I disembarked the shuttle at the Paris-Etoile Metro Station. Bought a first-class ticket to Le Gare de Lyon where I would connect with the TGV. A young English girl working in Paris guided me to the proper train, which she was also taking. She got off at Chantilly and I got off at the next stop, Le Gare de Lyon. I must say, the Paris Metro is  very impressive – clean, bright, plenty signage, on time and very efficient. I found the TGV (bullet train), bought a first-class ticket Paris–Nice (800F), waited, boarded and the train left as scheduled at precisely 10:41. I dozed off and on during the five hour trip. I was really tired and sweaty. The French countryside is so beautiful, especially between Paris and Lyon. Also I didn't expect the thrill of whizzing so fast (175 mph), almost silently, through the lush farmland and pastures. Arrived in Nice just before 6:00 and took a cab (50F) to the travel-book-recommended Hotel Georges. I was a little disappointed – not as "charming" as described. The propriataire was a lovely woman with a kind face, and spoke no English. She showed me a very nice room, clean and with a southerly view. I agreed and we went back to the small lobby to complete the paperwork. She saw I was from California and we chatted a bit about that. Then when I asked, she suggested a small restaurant nearby. This would be my first really French meal! Woo hoo!

Took a bath, relaxed, and decided now to go out to dinner. It was 8:30 and I was getting hungry. But I couldn't find the place she recommended and walked about a kilometer until I found another restaurant, but it looked dull. Walked some more and picked a restaurant called "Atmosphere" because they offered a Salade Nicoise. It was awful but the local wine was quite good. Yet, because it is my favorite salad, I am determined to search for the definitive Salade Nicoise at every opportunity. And then, hoping to find lodging that was a little more appealing, I walked to a hotel nearby, La Peronge, to inquire about a room for Thursday night, but no rooms were available. Inquired next door at Hotel Suisse. They had one with a sea view for a little less than Georges but I couldn't see it and the nearest parking was three blocks away. So I think I'll stick with Georges.

I walked back to Hotel Georges, got lost and ended walking an extra kilometer. It's now an hour past midnight and I was enveloped by the weariness of a very long day. I decided to sleep until I wake in the morning. And I think I'll leave Nice tomorrow when I pick up the car at the airport. And from what I've seen, Nice is a very, very beautiful city.

I woke up twice in the middle of the night with a headache and took some pills. Finally woke at 9 a.m. I think a half litre of wine while so fatigued was not a very good idea. But voila! Here I am in France, excited to begin this long awaited odyssey. I would have some breakfast and head to the airport to pick up my car. I was alone on the upper terrace having breakfast and noticed a construction project with cranes, etc. across the street. Its noise is what woke me at 9 o'clock. I then went to my room, packed, and read my guides till noon. When I went down to the lobby to check out, I was greeted by the propriataire with a worried look on her face. She nervously held up the morning newspaper with the banner headline *"TREMBLEMENT DE TERRE EN CALIFORNIE,"* (trembling of the ground) meaning earthquake! I took the paper and managed to understand much of what I was reading. It was the Loma Prieta quake of October 17, 1989 that struck the San Francisco Bay Area, collapsing freeways and bridges in Oakland and causing extensive damage and fires in San Francisco. I asked to call my son Jason who was living in San Francisco, but realized I had not packed his phone number. So I tried to call Nadene twice but didn't have the right number. Then I tried NY information for Eli's number but couldn't get them. Finally in desperation I called Carole, who drove to my apartment, looked up numbers and called me back at the hotel. We chatted briefly and I brought her up to date. The phone lines to San Francisco were jammed but I finally got through by early afternoon and to my profound relief, Jason was okay. He had been out taking pictures.

I thanked the propriataire as I left the hotel and finally found a taxi (50F) to the airport to pick up the car. I checked it out carefully in the parking lot, then drove back to the hotel (roundaboutly – missed the street), and picked up my luggage. And I thanked Madame once again. The little Renault is cute and well designed, drives responsively and smoothly, and gets great mileage (52 mpg). All instructions, etc. are in French. And to my happy surprise, they gave me a 4-door at no extra cost.

I headed east and drove through Nice and then through Villefranche, Monaco and Monte Carlo all the way to Menton next to the Italian border. Menton, where I stopped for lunch, is a lovely city with long sandy beaches and terraced slopes planted with citrus fruit and olives. I delighted in the many flowers everywhere. *Menton is a possibility.* I then turned about and headed west. My goal was to visit as many towns and villages as I could to find that unique place that resonates with my desires, the place where I want to live. My general plan was to zig-zag between the villages along the Mediterranean coast and the hill towns above, occasionally stopping along the way to walk about and sense their character and personalities.

Storied Monte Carlo and Monaco were impressive and exciting but more frantic than I could be comfortable with over time. Eze, a strange, isolated village way up on the mountain, was spectacular but limiting. As I continued westward, on through bustling Beaulieu, I drove down to St. Jean-Cap-Ferrat, a very small, quiet resort overlooking its yacht harbor. Not bad.

St. Jean-Cap-Ferrat

I then circled back to Villefranche, where I parked the car in a public lot. Villefranche is a small picturesque town that clings to the hills above even as it nestles around an important deep water harbor. It is a charming old city with narrow winding streets and steep walkways. Many small shops and cafes, and brightly painted houses line the waterfront. I located a bank as I needed to change money (1,200F). I had wanted to stay at the Welcome Hotel but it was full, so I got directions and a map from a real estate office to the Hotel Fiore. It looked pretty good so I checked in and was offered an attractive room with beautiful views of the bay. Dinner and breakfast is included at 420 F. I relaxed, journaled, and then went down to dinner.

Villefranche

Dinner was especially fine (pour le pensionnaire). Fish soup, quail, vegetables, ice cream, coffee (asked for "du café noir" and got espresso – wonder if that's typical – better to ask for "café sans lait?") And I managed the entire dinner without changing hands. Also had a 3/8 litre carafe of some good blanc de blancs (Cote de Provence). It was all so lovely, except the lighting was too bright – dimmers and candles on tables would have made a charming ambience. I was tempted to suggest it but wisely decided not to.

Hotel Fiore

The view from my window

I tried to do itinerary planning (finally) after dinner, but got sleepy and set my clock for an hour and a half nap (it's 9:30). I slept through the alarm but did manage to get up at 1:00 and worked on the planning till 6 a.m. Then back to sleep until 8.

I showered, dressed, and had breakfast on my small open balcony. The view out over the harbor couldn't have been more perfect. The water shimmered vividly in the bright morning sun, the small fishing boats were all still at rest, and there seemed to be a tranquil stillness in the air. In this lovely setting I began to plan my day.

I had a client who lived in Phoenix and had bought a house on the beach in Del Mar that I had designed in 1976. I did some work for him there and he thought very highly of me. He was involved in a major project being developed along the autoroute near Nice. The architects were American and European and their office was in a villa in Mougins, a small town in the hills above Cannes. When planning to leave, I had told my client that I was open to all possibilities, including architectural work. He arranged a meeting (interview) with the architects and gave me contact information. And so I called Tore from my room at Hotel Fiore and was told that he was out until 1:00. I said I will call back.

I walked around the old village exploring its narrow winding streets and stairways, its little shops and open markets. And I'd love to return later to a restaurant that advertized "La vraie salade Nicoise." Villefranche is a beautiful little port and very likable, and I would like someday to return. I imagine it's packed, though, in the summer.

Once again I phoned Mougins, talked to Tore, and made an appointment for 3:00. I headed back to Nice, but couldn't find the highway I was looking for (D35). I went too far and found myself in Antibes. I doubled back and found the road up into the hills to Grasse which then intersected D35 North of Mougins, so I took D35 down to Mougins. I inquired about the street I was looking for (the villa is not in the town proper but in its environs) and here it was, just two blocks away. I arrived at 3:00 and waited for a half hour; finally Tore came out with Peter Backe and Leif Johanson. [My portfolio would have been particularly useful but wouldn't have been worth dragging around]. They were neither gracious nor rude. They listened politely (Tore asked the questions) but seemed anxious to get back to work. They said they are not doing much now except waiting for approvals. I don't think anything will come of it, so I'll forget it. But it's still a bit of a disappointment.

I tried to find a hotel in Mougins and there are only two in the old village; one was closed, the other too expensive. Mougins is also notable because of its highly-rated restaurants. The old village is a walled city and very charming, but dull as can be – didn't really like Mougins.

So I decided instead to drive to Grasse (about 30 minutes). It was getting late and dark. Grasse is appealing and stretches out over the foothills of the high limestone plateaux and looks out over rich flowered plains. Grasse is particularly noted for its centuries-old perfume industry. In the old town, replete with narrow alleys linked by

104

steep ramps or steps, I found a brand new hotel. Slick digs, funky neighborhood (all the street lights went out at 7:30 – typical? or unique?) I was surprised by the very few restaurants around and had trouble finding one that had any character (Maestre Boscq, from my guide book was closed). I finally located a neighborhood eatery which was pleasant and not at all touristy. I stuffed myself with excellent cuisine and returned to the hotel, wrote a few notes and went right to bed.

Grasse

Altogether, this was a long, frustrating and dis-heartening day. Now I'm beginning to wonder if I really should be making this move. Traffic is thick and constant. People are everywhere – I can't seem to find the tranquility I'm looking for. But I must try not to get discouraged – tomorrow will be a better day.

I awoke at 3 a.m., wondering if my body clock isn't timed yet, but managed to get back to sleep till 8 o'clock. After showering and attending to my morning toilette, I went down to breakfast. Maybe because I'm becoming impatient and a little dispirited, I'm now considering if I should go directly to Aix. I already knew a lot about Aix-en-Provence. My children who had been there raved about its charm, its beauty and its way of life, so I may already be a little biased. I might revise my itinerary a bit, explore around Grasse for a while and be on my way. It's mid-morning on a bright, sunny, partly cloudy day – temperature in the 60s.

I had driven two kilometers before I realized I was leaving Grasse in the wrong direction. So I turned north onto the D2085 and was soon out of the town, intersecting the D6 and winding eastward through the verdant hills. I was reminded of many mountain roads I've traveled, twisting, narrow and with spectacular views. Then on the D2210 the terrain is semi-mountainous with deep gorges and steep hills. And into and onto these hills are built the most beautiful and fascinating villages, like storybook images. They are first seen from a distance, hugging the hill as if for dear life. And then in a wink, I'm creeping through the beehive of activity on the main street, and then fleetingly back out on the road and on the ramparts of the hill waiting for the next magical village to appear. There was Bar-sur-Loup, and then Pont-du-Loup, and the spectacular Tourette-sur-Loup. It was all so dramatic and incredibly breathtaking.

I wanted to linger, have a beer or café, but my outlook had been down and I was anxious to get settled in Vence, a small picturesque hill town about which I had read glowing reports. And yet this short drive of less than an hour raised my spirits and must have surely brightened my eyes.

It was about midday when I drove into Vence and purposely found the Centre-Ville (downtown). I parked, and with my list of researched hotels in hand, went hunting. My first choice, Auberge des Seignuers, was supposed to have closed October 15 and it did. My second choice La Closerie des Genets did have a room available with a sink and bidet, but no shower/bath, and the w.c. was down the hall. I looked it over, found it very appealing and took it, deciding to make the inconvenience a bit of an adventure. Besides, I could still pee in the bidet. Should I stand or sit? Hmm. The best surprise was 120 F. including breakfast, a third of what I'd been paying. This hotel couldn't have been more convenient right there in the middle

I unloaded my bags and feeling parched and a little weary, I went out to a nearby sidewalk café and leisurely enjoyed a beer.

 Then I drove about a kilometer down the hill to this revered jewel, Henri Matisse's prized *La Chappelle de Rosaire*.

It was a stroke of luck (or timing) that I didn't realize until later. The chapel is only open Tuesday and Thursday (and on other days only to tour groups), and I arrived just as a tour group had started. So I artfully slipped in and joined the tour. I had kept to the back of the group, and when they all left, I slyly lingered and had all the time I wanted.

The Chapel was built for Dominican nuns and completed in 1951. At the age of 77, Matisse had begun what he called the greatest project of his life. He spent more than four years working on the chapel -- its architecture, its stained glass windows, its interior furnishings, its murals, and the vestments of the priests. It also houses a number of Matisse originals and was regarded by Matisse himself as his "masterpiece." Here where the skies are so clear and so intensely blue as to be almost unnatural. It's a deep Matisse blue, without a trace or even a smudge of cloud, and of such crystal clarity that you can see forever.

When I returned to downtown Vence, walking around and absorbing its warm personality, I was looking in the window of a real estate office pricing apartments when an elderly man asked me if I was looking for an apartment. He had one for rent and would like to show it to me. I said OK and he got his wife and we drove (in my car) to see. It was in a newish building that he owned, 5th floor walkup, but with spectacular views – otherwise boring. I told him it didn't quite suit me and as we drove back to town he invited me to his apartment in town for coffee. I accepted, had coffee and cookies and both of them were so charming that I felt a little guilty. Then I realized that they needed this touching a fresh being as much as I did. We conversed, though clumsily, in French. Their name is Martowicz.

Upon leaving, I went on a leisurely stroll for a while, took a 30-minute nap at the hotel and went down to dinner at the hotel restaurant. Beautiful, charming room, what you think a French restaurant would look like. Soft Chopin, friendly service, great food. Many French restaurants offer a prix fixe multi-course meal which they call a "Menu." I ordered the Menu 100F. with andoillettes (sausage made the real way, with tripe innards and gut skins – new taste for me), canard l'orange, potatoes, ratatouille, cheese, raspberry tarte, coffee and half a litre of vin blanc. And the light. I loved the light here in the South of France, that clear yellow luminance that held everything in its crystalline precision, daring you to paint it or write poetry to it or at least cook a great meal and eat it outdoors.

Then after walking around town for an hour tuning in to its unique ambience, I stopped at La Victoire (hotel and patisserie) for a café and wearily returned to the hotel just before midnight.

I found Vence to be a <u>most suitable place</u>, definitely a possibility, although there doesn't seem to be much public nightlife. But nevertheless <u>very agreeable</u>.

Vence

At 8:30 on a beautiful Sunday morning I went out to take pictures for an hour and then returned for breakfast. I drove out to the Matisse Chapel again for photos as well as for a long view of the village. Alas, it was too late (11:00) – the sun had moved too far. So I went back to the hotel, loaded the car, bade Vence adieu, and drove 30 minutes on the D2 down the hill to St. Paul de Vence, one of the oldest medieval towns in the French Riviera. I found my first choice hotel on the outskirts of town, Le Hameau, and took a most delightful room and bath in a separate little building (like a casita), with a small terrace, 295F + breakfast 33F. What a lovely hotel with orchards all around and beautiful views.

Le Hameau

I took a five minute walk to the old city but did not enter. I rather sat on the terrace of the Café de la Place outside the ramparts of the old city to watch folks in their Sunday finery promenading and chatting on this warm and sunny day. In the meantime, I indulged in a couple beers and a dish of ice cream. But it's 2:30 now and I'm going to visit the Maeght Foundacion, open 2:30-6:00.

It was exhilarating to spend a couple hours there in those elegant buildings and exquisite grounds, viewing this incredible collection of work of 20th century artists, including Braque, Calder, Bonnard, Miro and Leger, as well as Chagall, Giacometti, Chillida and so many others.

I then returned to the hotel, took a 45 minute nap, and went into town for dinner. I walked around until I found a place that looked good (not much was open). The meal was so-so but the wine was excellent.

St. Paul de Vence is a walled city, not only physically but in other ways as well. It is like a package neatly wrapped in antiquity, with no apparent life outside its galleries, ateliers, shops and restaurants. I'm sure people live upstairs, but the village seems to totally close down at night. At 9 o'clock I'm walking alone along these cobbled, narrow streets listening to the echo of my own footsteps. Eerie. The box opens – the tourists come – it gets dark and the tourists go – the box closes. An incredibly beautiful place, reeking of history, but just as dead. At least that's my impression. Anyway, I walked back to the hotel, wrote a few notes, and planned tomorrow (maybe I'll take the long drive directly to Aix). And I need to study a little French.

St.Paul

After showering, etc. and while having breakfast I chatted with a couple from Palo Alto who were there enjoying their holiday. I finished coffee on the terrace and checked out of this lovely and most pleasant hotel. After getting directions to the A8 autoroute from the manager, I drove down the road and found the discount self-serve gas station, filled up, and saved 0.40F per litre (7 cents – wow!). As I headed toward the A8 at Cagnes-sur-Mer, I overshot the entrance, copped a couple of quick U's and properly entered the A8 heading west.

I must have really been anxious to get to Aix because I chose not to stop in Antibes or in Cannes, which is a large and bustling city. Cruising along the A8 I resisted the temptation to turn south to St. Tropez and a little farther to turn north to Draguignan in the hills. It was an easy and comfortable drive without much traffic. The directional signs are excellent and the highway is well maintained and nicely landscaped. I stayed under 110 kph (70 mph) as I watched very fast passers whizzing by. I went through two peages (tolls) and got to Aix in two hours. The entrance into the city is lovely – a tree lined roadway called Via Gambetta for about two kilometers, then onto the tree lined one- way ring road with three lanes of counterclockwise traffic circling the Centre Ville (old city). I finally pulled over and parked in order to buy a map because I didn't know where I was. However I then noticed that where I was parked was illegal so I drove around the corner to a public garage. From there I walked toward what appeared to be one of the few major entrances into the Centre Ville and where I sensed much activity. I must find a store where I could buy a map. I quickly found myself caught up in the mass of people – students, workers and others everywhere. It was 12:15 and the stores were closed so the map would have to wait. I continued to walk in this old and lively place, caught up in the flow of people moving purposefully somewhere, past a bubbling fountain or a grove of trees in a small Place (plaza) where some were sitting, chatting and lunching. And I was liking it more with every turn in the street. I had no idea in which direction I was headed or where I was going. I just let myself be 'lost' and swept up with the moving masses of people, going down this street and that, and feeding on the energy and vibrancy of this place. My children who had been here told me about the major heart of the city, one of the grand boulevards in the world, the *Cours Mirabou*. It is about a quarter mile long and lined with double rows of absolutely breathtaking 40-foot high plane trees (platanes) flanking the broad sidewalks on each side of the street. On one side are six-story institutional buildings with banks and business offices, and on the other are shops and the outdoor patios of the many restaurants. There are major fountains at each end of the Cours as well as a natural, still flowing fountain dating from Roman times at mid-length of the boulevard. But I wasn't prepared for the impact on my senses as I was swept by the throngs down a particular narrow street, and not knowing where I was, suddenly bursting onto the Cours Mirabou.

I was undone! Now in late October the leaves were turning red, orange and yellow and then falling to form a blazing carpet on the ground; and the midday sunlight filtering through the magnificent canopy was simply stunning. I recall so vividly that I stood there for a minute or two in the middle of this busy sidewalk, transfixed, and with my hands thrust deep into my pockets as I looked all about, saying to myself with absolute certainty,

"THIS IS THE PLACE!"

After a few minutes, I floated over to a small table at an adjacent sidewalk café, ordered a beer, and began to muse about my future here. I had essentially completed my primary mission and still had two more weeks left – a welcome opportunity to explore this city which will become my home.

Aix-en-Provence was founded by the Romans and is now a city with a population of about 124,000, plus about 12,000 students, who give the city a vibrant youthful energy. Aix has long been a university town, its colleges chartered in 1409. Today the University of Aix-Marseilles remains an important educational centre, specializing in humanities, law and economics, and with many teaching and research institutes. Places (plazas) with fountains or trees seem to be around every corner. Aix embraces art and culture with a passion. Paul Cezanne lived and painted here. The Vasarely Foundation built a new museum just to house his works and the Granet Museum features an extensive collection of fine arts and archeology. The many Festivals for Music and Opera feature some of Europe's best performers such as directors

Kurt Masur, Simon Rattle, the Berlin Philharmonic, the London Symphony Orchestra, Natalie Dessay in Verdi's LA TRAVIATA, and so much more. Many art galleries show outstanding work from throughout France as well as that of the many artists living here. The climate is temperate and flowers are everywhere. As rustic farmers sell their fresh produce under the shade of graceful plane trees, the markets teem with fruits and vegetables, olives, spices, cheeses, meats, poultry and all kinds of exotica. And the wine! The wines of the Cotes du Rhone are outstanding and most are reasonably priced. Provencal cooking is very distinctive from the rest of French cuisine. A Mediterranean influence brings recipes with seafood, lamb, fresh vegetables, garlic, olives and the abundant "herbes de Provence."

The region around Aix is replete with ancient towns, quaint little villages, farms and vineyards. Marseilles is 25 kilometers south, to the west are historical cities like Arles, Nimes, Salon, Avignon and to the southwest the renowned region of the Camargue. Across the Luberon Range to the north lie spectacular hill towns like Roussillon, Bonnieux and Gordes. All are within an hour's drive. The Provencal landscape is richly colored with wild sunflowers, lavender and red poppies. And the light, that fabulous light of Provence, its clear luminance holds

everything in crystalline precision, and with skies so clear and so intensely blue as to be almost unnatural.

I found a store open on the Cours and bought a map and a green Michelin. I located and walked to my first choice hotel just a few blocks away, and took a very nice room on the second floor overlooking the entrance courtyard (364F = $61). Le Manoir hotel is a restored and converted 14th century cloister. It is on a small sidestreet in the old section, very quiet, and just a four minute walk from the Cours Mirabeau. When I requested, they provided an extra table lamp. Armed with my trusty map, I walked back to the garage and retrieved my car. Driving back was an adventure negotiating the narrow

one-way streets. When I passed through the wrought iron gate and into the gravel courtyard and moved into my room, I flopped onto the bed and lay there a long while, musing on my extraordinary good fortune.

I soon needed to get out and stroll on this street and that, absorbing it all. I stopped for a beer at Longchamps, a sidewalk restaurant on the Cours, and watched the passing parade of gorgeous people. Walked some more, bought postcards, had ice cream, and then back to Le Manoir. A very good dinner was served at a small restaurant across the street (salad, red mullet, vegetables, dessert, vin, café (150F = $25).

After dinner I went back to the Cours, sat at a table at a sidewalk café and drank it all in. Now feelings of exhilaration mixed with questions and wisps of doubt flooded my mind. Do I really want to do this? Is this just a fantasy ambition and now that it's really before me, identified and possible, do I really want to do this? What will I really do here? All this while sipping a pastis, absorbing the energy and vibrant life all around me. Well, back to Le Manoir and new questions to ponder.

I was up at 8:00 still weighing it all. It's been a week since I left San Diego and most of my discoveries here have gone very well. I'm starting to get the rhythm of the place, and although I can't converse in French, I still feel confident and optimistic. This morning I passed up breakfast but bought a croissant and coffee at a sidewalk restaurant on the Cours Mirabeau. It was a beautiful morning, bright and sunny, as I sat there reading the *International Herald-Tribune* and watching the parade of lovely women and handsome men. Later, as I was keeping a journal, I made copies for letters and also bought envelopes. After returning to Le Manoir, I washed clothes at a nearby laverie and hung them to dry in the hotel room.

I went back to the Cours and at Les Deux Garcons had a Salade Nicoise. It was (just) OK. That was lunch, the first lunch all week. Breakfast and dinner had seemed to be enough. Then I did a lot more walking and exploring.

I stopped at a real estate office and made an appointment for 4:00 to look at an apartment in the Mazarin, an attractive area in the southern area of the Centre Ville that I had my eye on. I continued exploring the neighborhood until I met the agent to see the apartment: a third floor walkup with two rooms and a mezzanine. It also featured a leaky roof, a sloping floor, and a closet kitchen. The lav and bath were by the bedroom and the w.c. was by the front door – 4,000F per mo. Plus electricity and heating. I thanked him for his time and left, scratching my head.

Upon returning to Le Manoir, I sat down and wrote letters and then went out to buy stamps at Le Poste. At 8:00 I spoke again with the real estate agent and asked if there were rooms or apartments to rent for one or two weeks. He suggested the "Citadines," a residential apartment complex a couple kilometers west of the Centre Ville.

In the middle of an expanded Aix-en-Provence, about a kilometer all around, is the "old city," that is, the <u>Centre Ville</u>. This is the area that appealed to me most as the place to live, so full of character with its more than 200 year old 4-6 story buildings, narrow winding streets alive with bustling foot traffic, and everything within walking distance. Later that evening I had dinner at a pleasant little neighborhood restaurant -- good, plain, cheap. Then back to Le Manoir to finish letters and to bed by midnight.

I was up at 8:00 and had breakfast at the hotel. After getting additional copies of my journal for letters, I continued on toward the "Citadines." It would be a nice walk. But before I got to the end of the Cours, I stopped at another real estate office and asked the agent if he knew of a residential hotel or apartments to rent for a week or two. He suggested "<u>Hotel Particulier</u>" (an urban "private house" of a grand sort) on rue Clemenceau, just 20 meters from the Cours Mirabeau. I doubled back and found the address but all I could see were heavy bolted wooden doors, with a small push button call system on the side. No windows, no info or anything. I almost gave up, but scanning the names on the buttons, I looked up in my pocket dictionary a "name" on one of the buttons I had seen frequently: "accuil" means "reception." <u>Aha!</u> I buzzed and was admitted into a great dark hall, empty except for a marble slab off the wall to form some sort of a table, and a stairway at the end which I ascended.

On the next floor I was welcomed by a pleasant young lady who explained the system, and yes, she had a room (a studio apartment) that was occupied but would be available tomorrow. After knowing I was genuinely interested, she informed the young man occupying (apparently on a day-to-day) that he had to leave today. I could come back at 3 o'clock. When I returned, she showed me the studio and in spite of its being on the <u>fifth</u> floor (high ceilings, no elevator) I decided to take it. Minimum stay one week; 1,800F, 1,800 security deposit; day-to-day thereafter at 1,800 per 7 days. The place is simply great. A large window looks out over the narrow street below. The ceiling is sloped with roof beams exposed and painted white. The room is bright, has a bath, open efficiency kitchen and a foldaway sofa bed, a dining table, four chairs, a closet, a bureau, two small tables and lamps. I'm thrilled that this will be my "Studio" for the next lamps. I'm thrilled that this will be my "Studio" for the next couple weeks.
Terrific!

View from the window to the Roman Fountain on the Cours Mirabeau

With a bounce in my step I went to a nearby bank and cashed $700 = 4,200F (no fees). Then checked out of Le Manoir, leaving the car parked there for the time being. I ambled over to the Mazarin Quarter (that's where I'd like to live) to look around and stumbled on an interesting looking restaurant, "La Brocherie," where I had a marvelous lunch of six oysters, salmon, vegetables, the best mousse chocolat ever, vin, coffee – 134F. [I later saw I had it on my recommended list]. It's near the church St. Jean de Malte. I headed back to my car at Le Manoir, drove to my new Studio and promptly got lost. I parked and was going to portage from there when a cop came up and told me "this is a reserved space – you can't park here." But he gave me directions to where I wanted to go, which I did. I parked in a pedestrians only area with flashers going and I made two trips on foot to the Studio (1/2 block) with my luggage, which I placed in the Lobby. I then drove my car to the Mazarin Quarter and just as another car pulled out, parked on rue 4 Septembre, a street with unlimited parking. I walked back the three blocks to my Studio, hauled my baggage to the top of the world, unpacked and happily moved in.

It was now time for grocery shopping at Monoprix (a grocery/supermarket chain) on the Cours Mirabeau where I bought muesli, milk, cheese, coffee, Schweppes and beer. When I had put everything away and settled back, I excitedly felt I had already moved to Aix – that I wasn't in a hotel, I was in an apartment and I was going to fix breakfast for myself tomorrow. It felt OK. More than OK!

Then I tackled the postcards (14) including the translation into French (just for the heck of it) for my French speaking children. That took from 7:30 to 12:00. And I have to buy 4 more cards for tomorrow. Way too much time has been spent on communications. It's good to send notes to friends, but I've spent at least 10 hours. That's not why I'm here. Anyway, I had no dinner but when I finished the cards it was too late to go out, so I had some cheese and went to bed.

I arose early and cheerfully noticed that it's a bright, clear day – great for photos, especially early with the morning light. Breakfast can wait. I roamed the Cours Mirabeau and bought four more postcards. I explored and poked around and shot 1½ rolls of flea markets, flower markets, produce markets, miscellaneous streets, fountains and people.

Also mailed yesterday's cards at Le Poste. I bought a cheap little radio (190F) at Monoprix, returned to the Studio around noon and made breakfast (muesli, grapefruit, coffee). After writing the last four cards, I took a short nap. When I later went out to mail the cards, I stopped for ice cream at Le Grillon — three delicious scoops of chocolate (25F). And looking all about and absorbing the ambience of these ancient buildings, I noticed, gratefully, that there aren't any billboards or large signs in the Centre Ville to assault the eye.

I returned to the Studio to catch up on three days of journaling, and at 8:30 it was time for dinner. I looked for the restaurant "Charlotte" at Place Ramus, but it was gone. Instead I tried "Maximes", a "chop house." Maxime must also be a master butcher, as I marveled at watching him cut steaks and filets on his butcher block in the dining room. I ordered the 98F Menu and had, without intending to do so, a deliciously blended meal. First course was a mousse of four vegetables, each in its own layer, all together, with dressing. The flavor of each vegetable was too subtle for me to distinguish. Then I ordered "Arlequin." It was a very tasty meat loaf of beef and lamb wrapped with eggplant and with a tomato based sauce. Finally, a marvelous raspberry mousse swimming in a light chocolate sauce. And of course, vin. Thoroughly sated, I lumbered back to my Studio for a cafe and to write today's journal and by 11 o'clock I'm finally caught up.

I spent a most fitful night coping with a slight headache, and was up a couple times. I finally rose and showered. But I felt a little down — maybe it's the slight headache that casts a pall over everything, or maybe I'm having to face up to decisions — in any case it was time to call today a kick-back day. So I went out and bought a couple of pastries and a *Herald-Tribune*, came back to my lovely Studio, ate grapefruit, made coffee and spent most of the morning reading the paper.

I studied some French for a while, read travel guides about Aix, and thought about what I need to do. No decisions, just thinking, and I made a calendar for the next week and a half. I then thought about whether or not to go to services tonight (to make contact) and the only synagogue around is in Marseilles. When I checked out how to get there, I decided it was not wise to go exploring during the Friday p.m. traffic. Maybe I'll drive down tomorrow at my leisure.

I like this singular independence but I don't like the lack of contact with other people. I could never hole up in my own garret in a kind of isolation. I know that the language is a barrier now, but I need a breakthrough. The only commonalities I can think of are (a) architects – there is no association listed and I haven't gone around knocking on doors; (b) other Americans – I haven't encountered or overheard a single one since I've been in Aix, and (c) the Jewish connection – that's why I thought about services. There's nothing in the phone book about "Jewish" in Aix at all, and in Marseilles only a temple and a couple of agencies (listed in the yellow pages under "Culte – Israelite" followed by "Culte – Diverse."

I'd like to have some help and advice on the best way to rent an apartment, what bank to use, should I keep (buy) this car, buy another car later, have no car but rent one when I want to travel.

I don't think it's important to rent an apartment now. First of all, most are available now or within 30 days. I think a better plan would be to return to this Hotel Particulier for a couple of weeks when I make my move and find an apartment then. My stuff can be shipped to some holding address till I can pick it up. But I'd sure welcome someone here to assist me.

At about 4 o'clock and after a brief nap, my headache was gone and I decided to go out. It's a beautiful clear sunny day, temperature in the 60s and the leaves continuing to fall. After mailing the last of the post cards, I walked around the west edge of the Centre Ville, while exploring possibilities for dinner later. Back at the Studio I finished off the cheese and cashews (I hadn't had lunch). I read my French Diners book and went out to my first choice restaurant. But it was filled (a good sign), so I searched all over among many, many restaurants for another one that looked promising. Suddenly I came upon this little hole-in-the-wall that was particularly appealing, called "Le Dernier Bistro." A lovely intimate little place that seated 17 when full, and good looking men and women enjoying dinner. This evening I savored one of the best meals ever. The Menu 98F started with marinated chick peas, mussels, cold cuts, a marvelous salad with endives, and hot chicken livers with a piquant dressing. By the time I ate this (and not all of it) I was almost stuffed. Then came the entrée – steak with mushrooms. I managed about half. Finally a perfect chocolate mousse. Also half a bottle of good local wine (20F) and coffee (5F). Without question, I must return.

After dinner I went to a jazz club I had seen advertised – Le Scat, and was pleasantly surprised. A basement space with a good sextet playing in a cavelike atmosphere, well designed and filled with gorgeous, attentive people. Had a beer and stayed for two sets. The 60F ($10) included a cover charge, which was well worth it. I may go back Saturday night. It was 2 a.m. when I returned to my Studio and dived, exhausted, into bed.

I slept till 8 o'clock and when I stuck my head out the window was greeted by a cold, windy, damp day. After showering, I made coffee and had breakfast while writing yesterday's journal. At 10:30 I bundled up and ventured out.

My radio is cute and a piece of junk but is well worth the 190F ($32). There are two "French Cultural" stations that usually play classical music, and it's been a good background companion.

I spotted the French-American Guild but it was closed. Then when looking for a particular real estate agency whose ad I'd seen, I came upon Les Designers, a contemporary design and furniture store I had passed the night before while looking for a restaurant. I went inside, browsed for a while and chatted with Eric Pietra, a young gay designer who spoke English. As we became acquainted, I told him I'm an architect and that I'd like to meet other architects. And also that I plan to move to Aix.

Soon Silvie Aliotta, the owner arrived. She's slender, around 40 with big bushy mousy-gray hair, a great DeGaullian nose and a husky, smoky Simone Signoret voice. She spoke no English but Eric was an efficient translator. Together they arranged for me to meet M. Frapolli, principal of the largest architectural firm in Marseille, on Thursday, 2 November at 11:30 for lunch at Les Deux Garcons in Aix. They also arranged an appointment for me on Monday morning with Valerie Martin, Agence I.P.A. (real estate) to advise me on renting an apartment. And I'm invited to come back and visit with them Monday or Tuesday.

Well, this encounter sure gave me a lift, so after leaving, I happened through the market and bought three grapefruits and a bouquet of mixed flowers. Returning to my Studio (that is a tough climb!), I put the flowers into a pitcher. Some orange and yellow marigolds, red carnations, pink mums and a couple I didn't recognize. How gay and uplifting they are, so fitting for my welcome shift in mood.

I've decided to stay in Aix for the rest of my time here in order to get as grounded as possible, and there will be time for touristing elsewhere later. I have to get back to Nice on Tuesday 7 November to turn in the car, because I fly out of Nice at 0645 the following morning.

Getting hungry, I went out looking for a small café for a Salade Nicoise, but I spotted a little creperie, had a "Forestiere" (mushrooms, bemachel, gruyere) and a beer. Really good. The Nicoise will wait for another time. Returning to my Studio I stopped at Monoprix, bought some butter and cheese, and continuing on found a boulangerie and bought my first baguette! Also bought a *Herald-Tribune*. Back at the Studio I ate half the baguette, read the paper (not much to read) and took a 45 minute nap. When I woke it was raining. I struggled with the crossword puzzle for a couple hours and wrote in my journal until 8 o'clock. I was planning to go to the restaurant that was full last night but am not very hungry.

Instead I went out to go to a movie and although there are three multiplexes with 10 screens, they all broke about 9:15-9:45. So I decided again to have a Salade Nicoise. I picked a little restaurant and the Nicoise would have been quickly forgettable except I must remember it as the worst I've ever had (even substituted rice for potatoes). I got to the movies and for 37F ($6.16) saw Batman in French (excellent dubbing). A very small screen, not crowded, and I enjoyed the film because the simple plot was easy to follow. I'd like to see it again because I got only a little of the dialogue. The longest line at the box office was to see Indiana Jones – it stretched 200 feet, four people wide. And when I left the theatre at 11:30, there was a similar line for the next showing. I was tired when I returned to the Studio and went straight to bed, but with a bit of an upset stomach.

I must have needed the rest because I slept till 9 o'clock, and for a change took a bath instead of a shower. It's an overcast, chilly Sunday morning, and quiet as can be outside. Even at 10:00, hardly anyone is out. A few minutes later the church bells started ringing. I'm having a chilled grapefruit, the rest of the baguette and coffee. I will go for a drive today.

I spent the next couple hours in deep introspection and writing down lists and options. I was also able to think seriously during the long tranquil drive to Marseilles. Do I really want to go through with this? If I do, what do I do with the car? Once I start making friends, will the loneliness disappear? Will I be forever sorry if I don't? I need to make some decisions soon.

A one-hour outing to Marseilles turned into 3 1/2 hours. First, I headed the wrong way on the A8, and as I'm stopped on the side of the highway to get my bearings, a lady from Spain looking for Arles stopped also and asked me for directions. I advised (wrongly as it turned out) to turn around and go the other way. Once I managed to drive around 25 kilometers after starting, I had to guess as to which turn to take to Highway D52 (I guessed right). The drive to Marseilles was much longer than I anticipated, but it was so worthwhile driving through verdant hills and beautiful countryside. I got lost in Marseilles, bought a map at a Mobil Day & Night, and finally, after several wrong ways, found Blvd Ste. Marguerite. I was looking for the synagogue (#249) but, alas, never did find it. So I backtracked toward where the map indicated access to the A51 back to Aix. Got lost again. This time, bad map. Finally I spotted arrows to the A51 which took me right through the train station! I adroitly managed to get out of the taxi lane into the bus lane and ultimately escaped train station traffic. When I found the A51 arrows again, I was on my way back to Aix. Then an easy 20 minute drive. Once in Aix, I detoured, out of curiosity, just to see Le Pigonnet, a well known 18th century mansion set in two acres of exquisite gardens and chestnut trees, and converted to a luxury hotel. Then back to the Centre-Ville, where I found a good place to park three blocks from my Studio.

I desperately needed some contact with people, if only visual, so I went down to Longchamps, nursed a beer and sat in deep thought for a while. I later found a little bistro that showed "Bourride" on the outside menu (fish chowder that I'd been looking for, as I wasn't very hungry). Anyway, it was one of the courses on the 98F menu, so I ordered that, together with "charlotte de loup" (sea perch) and dessert and wine and coffee. But it wasn't "Bourride," it was "Buillade", quite something else, but good just the same. The loup was delicious and the dessert spectacular. Everything was so beautifully presented. What a lovely dinner. And when I ventured down a tight spiral staircase in the corner I discovered that the cellar has an even better, cozier ambience.

Le Bistro Latin
18, rue de la Couronne

It was well past 10:00 when I returned to the Studio, did a little journaling and soon went to bed.

I was up and showered by 7:30 and had grapefruit and coffee for breakfast. I puttered around until 9:30 and went to my real estate appointment with Valerie Martin, who showed me a nice apartment on rue Aude. Living Room, tiny kitchen, big dining room with windows on two sides, two bedrooms upstairs, bath, top of building, elevator -- 4611F ($770) <u>unfurnished</u>. (affordable) -- No parking.

I then bought a *Herald-Tribune* and enjoyed an espresso sitting outside and reading the paper. Later read some apartment ads in a real estate office window and went inside and made an appointment to see two apartments at 3 o'clock. I also stopped at the Air France office and confirmed my flight from Nice to Paris on 8 November.

For lunch I tried a creperie, and the crepe was just so-so. I then proceeded to walk around in areas I had not yet been, and after an hour or so I seriously needed to sit and rest. I gratefully found a bench on the Cours Mirabeau.

A man already sitting there was reading a *Herald-Tribune* (an English speaker!) so I struck up a conversation. His name is Dennis Stock, apparently a well known photographer and author (he referred me to one of his books in the bookstore). He has a house in Woodstock NY and just bought a house in Rousillon (north of Aix), his fourth house in Provence so far. He thinks Aix is the best city in France and he says I picked the right place. A welcome validation of my own instincts! He gave me much helpful advice on banks, cars, parking, etc. and most significantly, he told me about the "American Center." All together, a priceless 30 minute encounter. And little did I know that this "random intersection" would have such profound consequences.

I then went to my 3 o'clock real estate appointment and looked at a dreary second floor walkup – 4,700F. They didn't even have a key for the apartment. So I walked over to Les Designers to visit Eric and Mme (Sylvie). She was out so I chatted with Eric for quite a while. I invited him and Mme to lunch Friday. He also told me he talked of me to an architect friend of his in Aix and invited me to have drinks with them at 7:00 Thursday. Then he suggested that a friend of his has a villa with her family in which I might be able to rent some rooms. His description of an old 3-story country house up a long driveway, with a swimming pool and with a southward view of the city sounded too good to be true. We are going there tomorrow for lunch at 12:15. Also the woman has an apartment in the Centre-Ville. I feel like I'm becoming predisposed to liking the villa. Well, I'll see (it is an exciting thought). Even though it's not in the Centre-Ville, the idea of the villa is very compelling. So out of curiosity, I walked to the street where it's located and it's just 10 minutes away from the north perimeter of the Centre-Ville, 20 minutes from the Cours Mirabeau. I returned to the Studio all charged up. Then washed some socks in the sink and hung them up in front of the window. They should be dry by tomorrow.

I went back to Les Designers to confirm lunch for Friday but Mme had not returned, although she did phone in and thought Friday may be iffy. So I'll stay loose.

I returned again to the Studio, had a beer, and wrote in my journal. It was almost 8:00 and I was going to try again the restaurant Le Felibre that was filled Friday night. I was able to be seated and for the entrée I had "daube-grand-mere," a kind of pot roast served with polenta. And vin. Also their diverse salad and chocolate cake and espresso. Very, very good and worth the wait! I later lingered for a while on a bench on the Cours Mirabeau before returning to my Studio at 10:30.

Up at 7:30 on a bright clear day and again had grapefruit and coffee. Today, October 31, is the last official day of my marriage. Didn't think much about it although I did intend to deal with it today.

With much anticipation I went out to find the American Center that Dennis Stock had referred me to yesterday. It was about a two kilometer walk, past one of the university campuses, up and down hills. I talked to a gracious English woman there and learned it's mostly a teaching center and general clearing house. But she referred me to the Anglo-American Group of Provence (AAGP) for information on activities, contacts, etc. She also gave me a copy of their newsletter which included names and phone numbers of members heading various committees. On my way back I bought dentifrice at Monoprix and stopped at a bank and changed $100 to 604F. Back to my Studio to rest and change clothes for my big luncheon with Eric and the Villa Lady. I have high hopes, but.......

Alas, disappointment. Villa Lady (Catherine) was still out of town but I'm to check back at 5 or 6 o'clock with Eric. I had for the first time shed my trusty vest and was finally wearing my black (hard) shoes. I was more than ready and was more than a little let down. But I must learn to keep expectations open and a little fuzzy.

I had lapin (rabbit) for an excellent lunch at La Hacienda, a meat and potatoes kind of place – 51F, including wine. Then I went back to the Studio and napped till mid-afternoon. Later I walked to L'Ecole des Beaux Arts hoping there was an architectural school but there was none there. It's been kind of a strikeout day. I bought a baguette on the way back to the Studio since tomorrow is a holiday (Toussante – All Saints' Day). It was almost 5:00 when I returned and decided to call Carole. It was good to hear her and talk to her – maybe 20 minutes. Then I called Eric regarding the Villa: not possible today as Catherine is coming home late and he suggested I try tomorrow. In the meantime he and Mme Sylvie Alliotta are trying to set up a meeting for me with another architect for Saturday.

When I went out to locate the Theatre Municipal for the jazz concert tonight which I had seen advertized, I had forgotten my maps and got lost. Bumbled around in circles getting directions from different people until I finally found it. Lesson: <u>don't go out without my map!</u> Showtime is at 8:45.

It was about 7:00 when I returned to the Studio. I called <u>Helen Picard</u> of AAGP (I'd been trying all day). She briefed me on Aix, AAGP, and invited me to a coffee on rue Victor Hugo where members frequently gathered, and suggested I call <u>Judy Hawkins</u> about housing. I did and talked with Judy for quite a while, and we arranged for me to call her early the next morning.

Helen   *Judy*

I went to the jazz concert at 8:15 and while in line to buy a ticket, was approached by young man who offered to sell me his extra ticket (reserved seat 120F) for 100F. OK. Good seats, first balcony, fifth row in this funky 250-year old theatre restored 30 years ago but still with wooden floors, old movie seats and highly detailed interiors. The young man is a sports reporter for one of the two Aix dailies. He speaks some English, I some French, so we could manage to converse. The concert started at 9:20 featuring the Tommy Flanagan (piano) trio with Walter Mraz on bass and Kenny Washington on drums. They played two brilliant 75 minute sets and an encore. Great classic jazz for a wildly enthusiastic crowd of about 250 mostly young fans. When the concert ended about 11:30, I went back to my Studio, had a Schweppes and went to bed.

Today, November 1 is Toussante, a local holiday. I wanted to get up early and take a long walk on the "rue de Cezanne" eastward to Le Tholonet, relishing the morning light and blazing colors of autumn. Le Tholonet is a small village with magnificent views of Mont Ste. Victoire and the superb surrounding countryside. Two picturesque rivers meander between the vineyards and fields of wild flowers. Le Tholonet was one of Paul Cezanne's favorite places. Its red soil, grey rock and intense blue sky all complemented by Ste. Victoire , offer a palette of extraordinary colors.

But it dawned overcast and cool, so I chose not to go. Instead, I called Judy Hawkins and arranged to meet her at "La Belle Epoche" at 9 o'clock with Janelle, her six year old daughter. Judy is 40 and from Newport Beach. Her husband just started a new job last week at Unisys in Rancho Bernardo and Judy and Janelle will be following in December or January for a few weeks. They have been here four years and hate to leave, even for a little while. She says this is typical. She told me all about the AAGP group and it looks exactly like the kind of contact I've been needing. We talked extensively and coffeed till 11:30. After a brief errand, I was on my way to lunch about noon and passed Judy, Janelle and a young man named Peter sitting at a table outside Baskin-Robbins, waiting for Harold Smith. I joined them (never got to lunch, had an ice cream instead), and soon Harold, who lives up above Baskin-Robbins, came down to join us. He's a very nice, friendly Canadian physicist working for the French Nuclear Energy Applied

Research Agency. We visited for a while and arranged to meet at 2 o'clock at Judy's apartment and then we'll all go visit the cemetery where people bring flowers (mums) on this special day. But being anxious to know about the villa, I went back to the Studio and called Eric at his home in Marseilles. He had talked to Catherine and she had changed her mind about taking in a roomer, since she had just begun divorce proceedings and the perception of a single male tenant in the house could make for an unwelcome problem. So that was another disappointment. But I have to stay loose and try to develop as many options as I can.

Harold was already there when I got to Judy's apartment and she showed me all around. It will be available for 4,800F when she leaves. A very nice place on the sixth floor with elevator access, but much too big for me. We all went down and walked a few blocks to the Parc Jourdin and then through to the cemetery.

Le Parc

Le Cemetaire

Many of the tombs were above ground and were several hundred years old. It was all so very beautiful with flowers everywhere amidst the throngs of well dressed people. We then bought pastries on the way back to Judy's and had some coffee there as well. The three of us will have dinner at Sako-Thai at 8:00.

I met Judy and Harold at the restaurant – had a good dinner with excellent conversation. I returned to my Studio about 10:00 and read for a while before going to bed.

I was up early and made some coffee. I'm still rolling around my options for having a car when I return – lease, buy or what? So I started by calling Nice about buying. They said they are only an agency and I would have to call Renault in Paris, which I did. We talked for a long time, but still having unanswered questions, I said I would call back at 3:00.

I found the Salon de The on rue Victor Hugo where I am to meet members of AAGP. Helen Picard introduced me around to about a dozen very open and friendly people – Brits, Australians, Canadians, Americans and a lovely elderly French couple, the Bernes. It was exhilarating, finally, to engage in real conversations with likable people speaking English. Among them I met Lucien Racine, who is in the travel business and lives in Aix and New York. He and his wife are going to NY next week for 6-8 months and want to rent their apartment. I told him I'd call him later. Another member, Barbara Caruso from upstate NY had been on a tour bus three years before that made a brief stop in Aix and she was so smitten by this place she decided then and there to move here. Six months later she closed her life in NY and, with bag and baggage, she was here. She suggested that when I move, to bring my stuff with me, pay the extra fare, and not go through the hassle of shipping, etc. Good idea. Later I started to make lists of stuff to see if it n would be manageable. Looks like it is. She also told me she rents parking space in one of the public garages for 250F per month.

Yes, that would be the way.

I left a little before noon for the venerable brasserie Les Deux Garcons (built in 1792) to meet with Jean-Pierre Frapolli, the Marseilles architect, as arranged by Sylvie Aliotta of Les Designers. He was a few minutes late and was with his associate Bernard Carpentier. We had a drink on the terrace and began our acquaintance. M. Frapolli speaks no English at all, so Carpentier translated. Soon Frapolli and I went inside for lunch, as it was a little chilly outside, and Carpentier went back to work. Lunch was graciously served and was delicious (salad, steak, vegetables, vin), and Frapolli did most of the talking (in French). I managed to understand about half of what he said and could respond adequately enough. Mostly we talked about architecture, family, cities, history, French and American culture. He's a handsome man with flowing hair, a major moustache and finely chiseled features, 5'-10", slender, 53 years old. He has a flamboyant and "artistic" way. He left about 2:00 and I went back to my Studio, exhausted. It is very tiring to sustain concentration on the foreign language for so long. So I read the *Herald-Tribune* for an hour.

I then called Renault in Paris about possibly purchasing my car and talked for 3/4 of an hour. She was not much help, but will call me back later. After all this runaround and doing some calcs, I decided I would turn in this car and re-lease (maybe for six months) when I return. Paris called back and she explained why there was a difference in price. It mattered not anymore, because I'd decided not to keep the car.

I called Lucien Racine and made an appointment to see his apartment at 8:30 Friday morning. I also called Barbara Caruso and made a rendezvous for coffee at 10:00 later that same morning. Then I called Judy Hawkins and we talked at length about housing.

At 7:00 I walked over to Eric at Les Designers and we went to visit his friend Jean-Pierre Manfredi and Laurence (girlfriend) at their apartment. They are a very nice young couple and we had a good conversation, gratefully in English. He has a small practice and works out of this, his apartment. He also showed me pictures of a school he had designed (so-so). He's about 40, looked tired. She is cute.

I left around 9 o'clock, walked around the neighborhood for a while and had dinner at a forgettable restaurant. I soon found myself sitting on a convenient bench on the Cours Mirabeau where I could watch the many young people promenading, flirting and laughing joyously. I too was grateful for my good fortune just being there, and happily lingered until I returned to my Studio.

It's Friday morning, I was up early and ready to go by 8 o'clock. It was a 25 minute walk to Lucien and Olga Racine's apartment in a huge apartment complex (eight years old) called La Tour d'Aygosi. It was much farther than I would have liked but it would have been rude not to visit them. They showed me around and then I told them I preferred to be in the center of town. They are a very gracious couple and understood why I would like to be in town. I stayed for an hour and enjoyed a very pleasant visit.

Then I went to Barbara Caruso's for coffee at 10:00. It was chilly so instead of us going out, I bought some pastries on the way and she made some coffee and we visited in her apartment till noon. What a place! Something like this would suit me perfectly. Top floor with roof beams, living room, dining area, kitchen, skylight, teeny bedroom and a large bedroom with a beautiful terrace – wouldn't I love it! But just a fantasy. She bought it two years ago and spent $8,000 furnishing it. She got most of her furniture and stuff at IKEA in Marseilles. She loaned me her catalogue. She talked about her trip to Venice tomorrow and I gave her some hotels to check out. She shared some of her moving-in experiences, talked of banks, parking, etc. She's a lovely woman, in her late 50s, and now a dedicated expatriate. I invited her to dinner this evening at 7:30.

Zipped over to Les Designers. On the way I made dinner reservations at Le Dernier Bistro for 8:00.

I picked up Eric at noon and we walked over to Bistro Latin for lunch – ate downstairs. Very nice. He had not been there before and liked it. After lunch he went back to work and I went to a bank to change some money ($200 = 1,200F). I returned to the Studio, did the crossword puzzle and took a short nap. I also browsed through the IKEA catalogue (which I would return to Barbara at dinner). IKEA stimulated a lot of new possibilities. Maybe I could go to Marseilles tomorrow.

Checked in with Judy and got the name of Nicole Girard who has an apartment to show me on rue Cardinale. She'll be in Monaco until late afternoon Monday. I'll call then or Tuesday morning.

I dressed for dinner – suit and tie (finally) and picked up Barbara who served aperitifs before we left. We walked to the elegant restaurant, and we both enjoyed the intimate ambience and the excellent cuisine. I had lapin. We returned to Barbara's, had a cognac and more conversation, and I returned to my Studio around midnight. And went right to bed.

First thing in the morning I called Renault at the Nice Airport to make an appointment to return the car on Tuesday November 7 at 5:30 p.m. I then called Judy and as she had no plans for this morning, we arranged to drive down to Marseilles. I hurried out, bought a pain chocolat at a patisserie, and ate it on the run. I jumped in my car, picked her up and we drove to IKEA. What a huge warehouse of furniture and furnishings, most pretty well designed, priced for the mass market. They sell everything, including plants. And I picked up my own catalogue. Mulling over my options I may...

    a)   Rent unfurnished, and furnish totally (including refrigerator, stove, lights. etc.)

    b)   Rent furnished

    c)   Rent furnished and augment with new bought stuff that I should be able to sell at half off when I leave. This is my current inclination.

We had a cafeteria lunch at IKEA and returned to Aix about 2:00. I then went to Les Designers but they were closed so I returned to my Studio. Eric called at 2:30 to tell me that he has set up a meeting with Jean-Pierre Garnier and his wife Charmi (also an architect) for 4:30.

I had time to go to Maurice and Denise Berne's open house and to join others there – the format is to speak French whenever possible. The Bernes are a delightful, lovely couple well into their 70s, and so sweet and kind and helpful. Maurice still calls her "my fiancée." I stayed for an hour and the conversational format seemed to work well. Elizabeth somebody showed me an apartment across the street (awful): one bedroom with the window on a stairwell.

I walked to Les Designers at 4:30 and met with Eric, Jean-Pierre, Chami and Mme Aliotta till 6:00. Eric invited me to lunch at his home in Marseilles tomorrow (Sunday). When I left I walked around their neighborhood looking for a restaurant for dinner (I had invited Judy and would call her). But I wasn't having much luck finding something, and I couldn't find the one Barbara Caruso had recommended, when I bumped into Judy and Valerie O'Neil, a photographer who lived in the Bay Area who now lives in Eguilles. They had just bought some pastries and invited me to join them for tea at Judy's. I suggested that my place was much closer, and since we were standing right in front of a store that sold tea, I bought some and the three of us repaired back to my Studio for tea and pastries, and I then invited both to dinner.

We left about 8 o'clock and cruised around until we found a simpatico place – Les Halles. It was festive, with live music and exceptionally good food – enough to keep us there for three hours. I had escargots (frogs' legs). We had two bottles of wine and a fine time, except Judy got sick -- was in the john for about an hour (Valerie checked up on her from time to time), while Valerie told me her love story – husband, French lover, past history, etc. She has some important decisions to make.

When we all left it was raining. We walked to the Pasteur Garage and got Valerie's car, took Judy home (she was not well at all) and Valerie dropped me off on the Cours Mirabeau at my street. When I got upstairs and hadn't even closed the door, the phone rang. It was Carole. The timing was uncanny. It was 12:30 a.m. here, 3:30 p.m. in California. We talked for about half an hour as she brought me up to date on some local matters. She had just received my post card (mailed nine days earlier). And then, after a very long day, I finally went to bed about 1:00. But I woke up at 3:00 with a stomach ache. I anticipated diarrhea and nausea like Judy, and went to the bathroom to await the worst. But there were no serious reactions so I went back to bed, wondering what we ate in common that made us both sick. And after all that I slept OK.

When I looked out the window at 7 o'clock in the morning, it was overcast and drizzly – not at all a day for walking the Route de Cezanne to Le Tholonet (I've been trying for a week). So I rolled over, went back to sleep and languished in bed till 10:00. The main things to do today are

    a)   hike out to Le Tholonet – well, that's out
    b)   catch up on miscellaneous papers, notes, journal, etc.
    c)   go to Eric's for lunch in Marseilles

And I felt fine, not sick at all.

Judy called just as I was sipping some coffee and reported that she too felt fine. She also had talked to Valerie, who had been sick in the middle of the night. Les Halles, in spite of its festive ambience, is now on my don't-go-there-again list.

In the meantime I washed socks, poured another cup of coffee and ate leftover pastries and a little cheese. I worked on miscellaneous stuff till 1:00. I then called Eric and told him I'm on my way. He gave me clarified highway directions. They were good, too, because I got to his neighborhood easily. I just couldn't find his house (I had forgotten that he'd given me the address – I found it later). After 45 minutes of wandering around his neighborhood on foot and by car, I called him from a gas station and he came down and got me. When we got to his place, he parked right where I had parked earlier while searching on foot. Two of his friends were there, Antoine, who works in a factory in Marseilles, and Catherine, a photographer from Paris here on assignment, whom Eric met last May at the Cannes Film Festival. Later Frederic arrived, also from Marseilles, 29, not sure what he wants to do. Lunch was so elegantly served and was especially delicious. Eric had prepared whole Truite de Mer, salade, cheeses, and provided three bottles of wine. Also an exquisite dessert. He has a fabulous place – one of four flats in this old chateau, and he is slowly putting it into shape. It commands a breathtaking view of the Marseilles harbor.

We had good long talks, mostly in English. I left about 6:30 with Antoine as my guide to the autoroute. First I rode with him on the back of his motorcycle down to where my car was parked, then followed  him to the entrance to the autoroute. I got back to my Studio by 7:30 when Judy called and invited me to come over to talk. I was a little weary so I declined and told her I had to work on my journal (which is true). I will see her tomorrow as she will introduce me to her banker, real estate agent, etc. I had some ice cream and by 10 o'clock I was caught up with all my journaling. But I've got to start making some lists. Tomorrow is my last full day here.

Up at 7:30 on a beautiful, crispy clear day. And it's cold (6 C. -- 42F.). I decided now to take that long deferred walk to Le Tholonet along the Route de Cezanne. I've been waiting for a bright sunny morning and, so very timely, here it is. And although this is my last full day in Aix and I have a lot to do, I'd always regret it if I didn't take this excursion. I've been in Aix two weeks now and it's gone by so very fast. I haven't done any of the touristy things, etc. but that can wait. I brewed some coffee and then called Judy to postpone introductions till noon.

I was on the walk by 8:30 on this very chilly morning. I wore three long sleeve shirts under my vest and removed one on the way. The street leads east into the morning sun and soon becomes a country road lined with trees and marvelous vistas. Soon it begins to descend, winding and twisting, into what appears to be a valley. There are small farms, chateaux and villas. The views, seen through back-lit trees, are breathtaking. Occasional glimpses of Mont Ste. Victoire are stunning. Suddenly these long rows of trees appear in the distance before me, brilliant in red and orange, stretching all the way across my view.

It was incredibly beautiful. Soon I am at the trees, and it is Le Tholonet, with Aix 3½ miles and 100 minutes behind me. I was going to hang around 20 or 30 minutes and take the bus back, but as I walked into the tiny
"town", two shivering people were standing, waiting for the bus. I asked them when it is coming and they said any minute, and lo, there it was.

I decided to stay an hour until the next one. So I wandered around, took some pictures, stopped at the "Relais Cezanne" and had a croissant and coffee. It was still cool and quite windy – and the air was crystal clear. The falling leaves of orange and brown were alternately fluttering and swirling. Soon the bus came and I got back to the Studio just before noon.

I called Judy to meet at Les Deux Garcons for a pastis. We ended up instead at La Belle Epoque where there is an outdoor heater. We had salades for lunch. While we were on our way to introductions we ran into Jerry and Claudia Weisberg from Ithaca NY who were on my list of people to talk to. They've been here 14 months and are returning. They are also staying temporarily at Hotel Particulier so I told them I'd stop by later to see them.

Judy and I continued on to the bank but her friend wasn't there today. We then went to the real estate office and I met Emmanuelle. Helen Picard wasn't home. Neither were the Bernes. I would like to use them as references on my visa application. Judy went home and I went to Les Designers and said goodbye to Eric and Sylvie. They would be most happy to serve as references. Then I made reservations in Nice for tomorrow at the Holiday Inn (595F). I visited the Weisbergs downstairs. He's an architect, builder and developer who sold everything, came to Aix on a sabbatical and is now returning to NY. They offered much good advice on car, apartment, furnishing, visas, etc.

I then made an appointment with Nicole Girard to look at an apartment at 18, rue Cardinale for tomorrow at 9:00 a.m. When I called the Bernes, they (Denise and Maurice) said come right over. I was there for over an hour, had the most delightful visit with this warm and charming couple. And they would be happy to be a reference.

I returned to the Studio and called Helen Picard. She's the president or something of AAGP. We talked for a long time, I told her my story, and she too would serve as a reference. I ate dinner across the street at Chez Antoine (a trattoria) -- not very special for my last night in Aix, but I'll be back. Arrived back at the Studio at 10:00, made the last of the coffee and read the paper. I was just too tired to pack – I'll do it in the morning. And I sank into bed at 11:30.

Well, these last three weeks have just flown by, and now it's time, and I'm leaving Aix today. It's Tuesday November the 7th. I woke at 6, was up at 7, showered, etc. Had no coffee this morning, but ate leftover chocolate ice cream for breakfast. It didn't take long to get all packed. I left at 8:45 for my meeting with Nicole Girard. I carried the big bag two blocks on the way to the car. I waited impatiently for Nicole because I had a lot of things to do this morning. Twenty minutes late, she showed me a teeny bungalow in the back that was cute but too dark and too small (2,000F). Then a big enough but ugly apartment on the fourth floor, awful green carpet, brown striped walls, partly furnished (4,500F). Finally her own occasional apartment up a narrow spiral stair to the fifth floor that was bright, sunny, two terraces, views, mezzanine, but needs a lot of work. It would be fine except for the long (but manageable) climb up the very narrow stair access. However, she doesn't want to rent it for longer than a month or two.

So I picked up Judy, went to her bank, met and got useful information from Andree. Then back to my Studio where Judy and I talked at length, finished the cheese, two beers, two Schweppes, and the semi-soft ice cream (like chocolate mousse). I gave her the rest of the leftovers and the powdered soap and the radio. After she left, I paid the balance of the hotel bill (620F telephone), and went out to buy picture post cards but decided not to.

I left this fine hotel with my green bag and loaded it into my car, stopped for gas and left Aix at 1:30. It was a pleasant drive to Nice, but I did not see an airport exit sign on the autoroute. I exited when it seemed I had gone too far, doubled back in city traffic and found myself on a street I didn't know. I stopped at a bus stop and on their wall map found that I was just two minutes from the airport. I drove around and found the Hotel Campanile, checked in (320F) and cancelled my reservation at the Holiday Inn. [Judy had called the Campanile to find out their rates and suggested I try there first – good idea – saved $40]

Then I returned the car without any difficulty, and took the ten minute walk back to the Campanile. The bar was closed till 7:30, so I walked over to the Holiday Inn and had a cocktail. When I came back to the Campanile I read the paper in the lobby, and went to dinner there at the hotel. The menu looked good but the food was dull. And, alas, my quest for the definitive Salade Nicoise will have to wait for my return. I went up to re-pack and went to bed at 10:30.

I rose at 4:30, showered, etc. and checked out of the hotel at 5:30. Then took a taxi to the airport, checked in at Air France, boarded with my two carry-ons, and left on time (0645). Looking out the window as we took off, I could watch the French countryside shrinking below me, and I was filled with such complicated emotions and anticipations of what is yet to come. I felt incredible optimism, with no trepidation or anxieties or second thoughts. I'm determined and excited about making this move and secure in the belief that it is just what I need at this juncture in my life. And that I'll be enriched by this stimulating new adventure. As I gaze out the window at France receding, I reflect about how, through a series of random intersections, I have managed to make a precious French connection and at the same time a valuable English speaking one as well. I know these opportunities will serve me in good stead. And what other chance encounters lie ahead for me when I return? I am so very eager to begin this next adventure.

We arrived at Terminal B in Paris at 8:20, and I used the free baggage carts to wheel over to Terminal 2A, where I got my ticket at Jet Tours, and checked in at Air France. I stopped for a croissant and coffee and wrote Monday's journal while waiting. We boarded the 747 at 10:15 and left at 11:00 (1/2 hour late). 3½ hours into flight I had a pastis, and then lunch. Now that I've had a steady diet of French food for three weeks, the airplane meal, though tasty, seems not as good as when I flew over. I did a little reading and wrote Tuesday's and today's journal.

The flight is only partly filled. I'm in seat C and the woman in seat A left to find an entire middle section to stretch out, so I have all three seats – aisle to window. It helps a lot. I talked off and on to a lady from Yugoslavia across the aisle on her way back to Washington DC. I read and then dozed for half an hour. They served a small lunch about noon (NY time) prior to landing at JFK at 1:15. I breezed through Customs (no look), took the Carey Shuttle to the Port Authority on 8th Avenue and 2nd Street ($9.50) and a taxi to the Hotel Excelsior. I checked in at mid-afternoon, unpacked, and went over to see Eli and Pauline at 3:30. The weather is cool and overcast and it was raining by 6 o'clock.

It's good to be back and see the kids. But these last three weeks have been intense, productive and incredibly enjoyable. My "mission" was successful and the heady anticipation of actually moving to this stimulating place in France that suits me so well is moving closer to reality.

As I think back on my madcap adventures over the last three weeks and all the glorious discoveries I made and all the fine people I met, I'm especially excited to begin planning the Big Move. Aix is magical and seductive, and its remarkable distinctiveness contributes so enormously to its ambience and unique identity. It's no wonder that people love living there. And I will too.

LEN VEITZER
June 2011

THE PERFECT EULOGY

Nadene and I were married about a week when we loaded up the Plymouth and headed east from New Orleans on the way to Florida. It was early May in 1957 and already hot and humid when, after a full day's drive, we rolled into Sarasota. After the night in a motel we sought out more permanent lodging and found an uncharacteristic log cabin alpine cottage on a half acre property. We quickly settled in and then drove into the village because I was bent on finding a job. Sarasota had become a hotbed of contemporary architecture and I wanted to taste some of it. I was an experienced draftsman, could work anywhere and was quickly hired. Nadene found a job as well. We were all set.

We both wanted to have a dog and after about a week we decided to get one. Nadene's family always had a dog and though I had wanted one, my family never did. So now the stage was set for our first compromise. She had always had a small female dog and I wanted a large male dog. So after much discussion we decided on a large female. On the next Sunday morning we checked the ads in the local newspaper and found *"Boxer and collie pups, 6 weeks old, male and female, $35 each"* and the address. This sounded appealing so we drove way out into the countryside to this large property with a house in the distance. As soon as we parked and got out of the car we saw these two yapping brown blobs bouncing out to greet us. Neither was a boxer nor a collie. But they were so excited and so very, very cute. The owner followed and confirmed that they had all their shots, etc. and were in fact a mix of boxer and collie. Imagine that! They were healthy and frisky and so happily frolicking together that Nadene and I conferred and for a brief moment thought about getting both. Prudence prevailed and that notion quickly passed. So we bought the girl and brought her to her new home.

Now, what should we name her?
Corny trick with dog:
"What's your name?"
"WOOF !!"
And that is what we would call her.

151

Nadene and puppy Woof in Sarasota

In September of 1957 Nadene and I left Sarasota for Miami to fly to Havana for a couple weeks to visit some of my relatives there. We put the car in a storage garage and Woofie in a well-rated kennel. When we returned we retrieved the trusty old Plymouth and a very excited and happy dog, and we headed north. The car was packed with all our belongings. The back seat was filled as high as the backs of the front seats. On top of all that I had placed my 42x30 drafting table top covered with a blanket. A perfect place for Woofie to lie and look out the windows.

The three of us stayed in motels along the way. On a hot summer day in Washington D.C. while crawling along in busy traffic with the windows open, Woofie is lying on her flat bed behind me. Suddenly, because of the traffic, I had to hit the brakes hard. Woofie and the blanket slid right past my ear and out the open window next to me. She landed on the pavement, startled and dazed but no worse for wear. I opened the door, retrieved my shaking pal and her blanket and put them back on the drafting table. She chose to retreat to the opposite corner away from any open window and preferred that for the next two days.

When we crossed the Hudson River through the Holland Tunnel into New York I had no idea where we were. We needed to find lodging, like a motel. So I turned left at the first traffic light on what happened to be Riverside Drive. And on and on we went with no motel in sight. It never occurred to me that New York City wouldn't have any motels. The scenery was beautiful and Woofie was enjoying it all from her perch above the back seat. But we needed to alter our plans and after a couple miles we spotted a tall building, the Paris Hotel, that looked pretty nice. We were relieved that they could accommodate pets and were assigned a room on the eleventh floor. We were worn and weary after the long trip from Florida and glad to be temporarily settled. But alas, a minor disaster struck. The next day Woofie, unsophisticated with city ways, pooped in the elevator. Of course they asked that we leave but with our embarrassment and pleadings the manager relented and consigned us to using the freight elevator.

A few days later we found permanent lodging in an apartment at 239 East 60th Street, a fourth floor walkup, consisting of a living room, a bedroom, a bathroom and a small kitchen. A really small kitchen. It was four feet wide and six feet long, which accommodated a prefabricated unit with a sink, a stove top, an undercounter refrigerator and cabinets above. The aisle was just two feet wide and only one person could be in there at a time. When we fed Woofie we put her dish at the far end of the aisle and when she was finished she just couldn't turn around. She had to put herself in reverse and back out and couldn't understand why we couldn't stop laughing.

Woofie grew into a remarkably beautiful dog with the fortunate genetic combination of the two breeds. A little larger than a boxer and with short hair of a golden brown hue. We didn't clip her ears or bob her tail. She had the large chest tapering to the slim body of a hound. Her muzzle was neither long and pointed like a collie nor flat and ruffled like a boxer. It was in fact of medium length, much like that of a German Shepherd. And she was frisky, smart and easy to train.

Woof and Len in Central Park

I would take her for a walk first thing every morning and as soon as I got home from work in the late afternoon. She would hear me coming up the stairs and would excitedly greet me as I opened the door. As soon as I picked up the leash she would bound past me, race down the three flights and wait at the front door. When I clipped on the leash and we went outside she immediately headed to the curb. Together we learned to abide by the signs to "Curb Your Dog." The sidewalks were always filled with fast-walking people. Our only urgency lay with Woofie and she learned quickly about what she had to do. But she was an unusually beautiful animal and people noticed. I was frequently stopped and asked about her breed and when I responded with the unusual "equal parts boxer and collie" folks were surprised but effusive with their admiration. But one time a well-dressed matronly woman in shocked surprise exclaimed, "Then she's not a *real* dog!" Hmmph! So I invented a new breed and Woofie became an "*African Veldthound.*" This seemed to satisfy the admiring curious and I always smiled so proudly. Then one day a woman excitedly remembered "Oh yes, I saw an *African Veldthound* last year at the Westminster Dog Show." I think I'm getting used to New York where nothing now surprises me.

On weekends it seemed we walked all over Manhattan, Woofie on the leash and discovering all kinds of new smells and sounds and the density of so many people. On Thanksgiving weekend we drove up to Boston and again couldn't find a motel. We ended up in Salem for the night, several miles out of town. Back in Boston it was freezing cold and after a couple hours walking about we would need to return to the car to warm up. We were bundled up from top to bottom and Nadene had gotten a sweater-jacket for Woofie, so the three of us managed to weather the weather. In the meantime Woofie was growing. And growing. And the cute little puppy was becoming a real beauty.

Woof and the Monster in front of the Plaza Hotel on 59th and Park Ave.

Occasionally during the winter New York City was blanketed with snow. On a Sunday we'd find a parking lot and Woofie would go nuts leaping and bounding and burying herself in the snow. And all through the winter the three of us would continue to walk everywhere.

We all left New York in late May of 1958 and arrived in San Diego four weeks later. Nadene was pregnant with our first child as we camped out at the Feilers (Nadene's parents) while searching for a home of our own. Here our Woofie met little Sheba (their dog). The two got along just fine and happily frolicked together in the large yard.

In our home on Russmar Drive Woofie would normally sleep on the floor at the foot of our bed. After Ian was born he slept in a bassinette also at the foot of the bed. A week after we brought him home I woke in the middle of the night to go to the bathroom. It was pitch black dark and as I inched past the bassinette Woofie awoke, startled, growling and snarling with bared teeth. I managed to speak quickly and calm her down and told her what a good dog she was. And I really meant it. It was profoundly comforting to know how instinctively protective she was and would always be.

Ian and Woof in Balboa Park

She adapted easily to our new home and was perfectly happy to rule the backyard. Eli was born a couple years later and Maia three years after that. Woofie took it all in stride. They were hers and she was theirs. In 1966 when we moved to Redding Road, Seth was born followed by Jason a year and a half later. Our family was complete and Woofie was a very happy dog. She was an integral part of the family and the bonding was priceless.

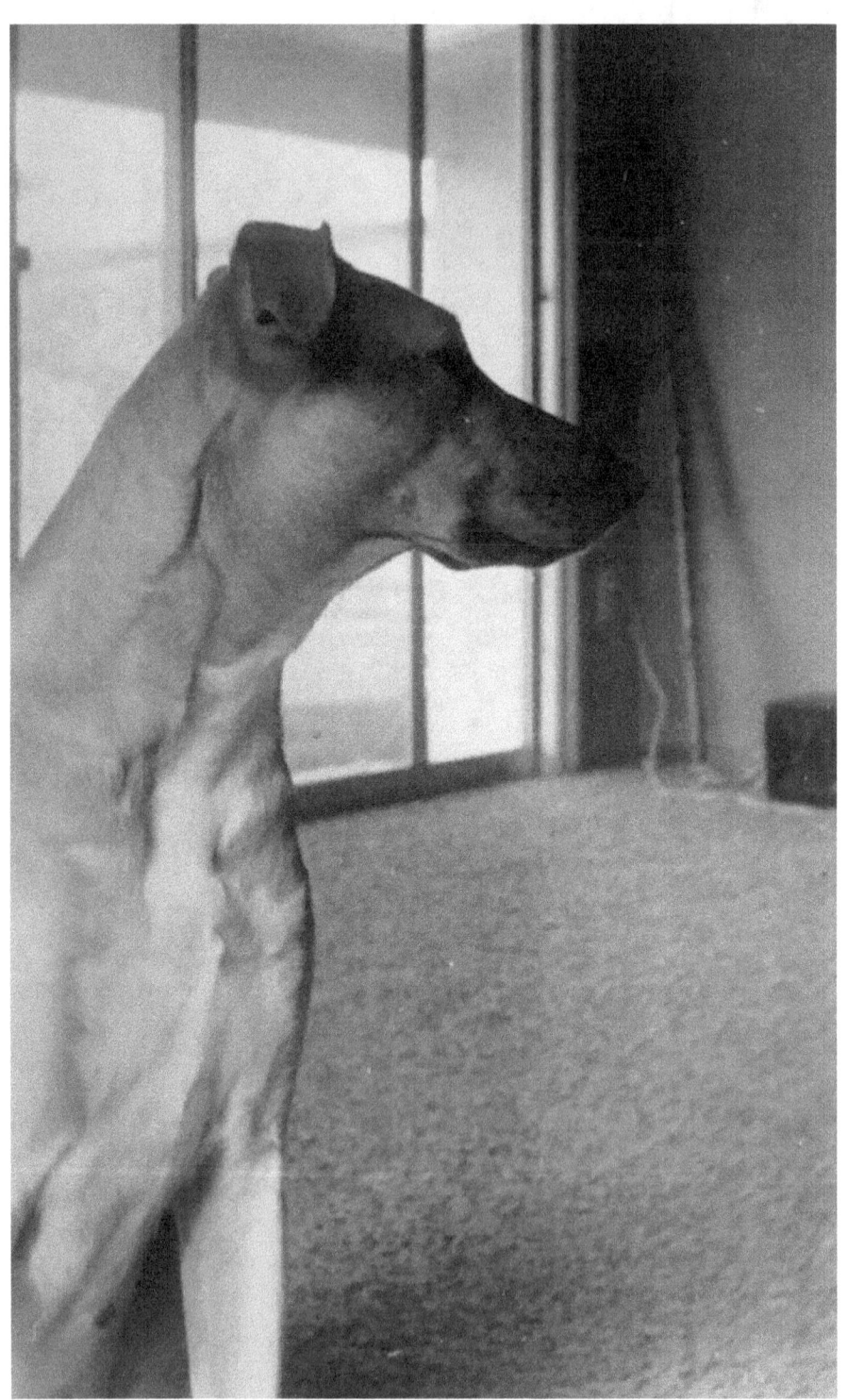

Little by little over the years she began to slow down and by the time she was getting close to 14 years old she had become more and more feeble. So sad to watch this inevitable decline. She had always been a happy dog and her protective instincts were as keen as ever.

I would normally come home from the office between 5:30 and 5:45 while Nadene was preparing dinner, and by 6 o'clock every day the whole family would be gathered in front of the TV to watch the *CBS Evening News with Walter Cronkite*. Then the seven of us would sit around our large round table in the kitchen for dinner.

Nadene's voice was trembling when she called me at the office late one morning. Woofie had just died. I came home immediately and through anguished tears caressed her gently and took her still warm body outside, cradling her so tenderly, and covered my dear, gone friend.

Seth was five years old and it was just past noon when he came home from kindergarten at Hardy School. When he came in he knew something was wrong and when we told him he broke down in tears. Then that sweet dear boy looked up at me and with tears streaming down his cheeks he asked, sobbing, "Will it be on the Walter Cronkite News?"

LEN VEITZER
May 2017

MY LITTLE RED WAGON

On a sad and fateful Monday morning many years ago I lost my sweetheart.

That is to say, simply, my car was stolen. Or not so simply. It was not just an ordinary car. Not at all like all the other cars I've ever had. This one was genuinely exceptional. For the past 18 years it had become an unconscious, inseparable part of me, like a favorite sweater or a personal talisman. My precious 1965 Alfa Romeo Giulia Veloce convertible was gone.

This was an extremely rare car. Out of many thousands, only 1,063 of this particular model were built in 1964 and 1965. It was powered by a four cylinder, 1600 cc engine with overhead cams and twin Weber carburetors. Its elegant, perfectly proportioned body was designed by the iconic Pininfarina, designer of Lancias, Ferraris and Maseratis. And like all truly genuine Italian cars, my Alfa was born red.

I immediately reported the theft and two officers came to interview me. I timorously asked about the likelihood of recovering the car, and as I expected, they said close to zero. I was heartbroken.

Some eighteen years earlier in 1970, Dale Shoupe, a dedicated mechanic who specialized in Alfas and Jaguars knew of my interest in Alfas and introduced me to Gary Lichty, a Navy man who was being transferred to the East Coast and needed to sell his Alfa. He had bought it in San Diego, added many upgrades, and had it meticulously maintained for the next four years by Dale. It was in absolutely perfect condition. For me, it was like love at first sight and I bought it for $2,000 ($12,000 in 2014 dollars).

Soon after, I bought a silk scarf, relishing the self image of me tooling down the highway with the white scarf billowing out behind me like in a World War 1 Sopwith Camel or a Gran Prix Formula 1 race car. So off I went in gleeful anticipation, but quickly discovered, to my chagrin, that the windshield and the body contours of the car shaped the air currents so as to blow the scarf forward instead of behind me. Couldn't see and almost crashed.

The top was always down except for rainy days. We rode majestically, my Alfa and me, knifing through the wind, hair flying, engine purring at 3,000 rpm, connected to the roadway and to the luminous sky above and literally to the world around us.

This was my everyday transportation. Each morning to the office and back. Driving to meet with clients, attend meetings and other business needs, day and night. Frequently, on my way home from the office, I would pick up my two oldest sons, Ian and Eli, from Hebrew School, straddle them both in the passenger seat under a single seat belt, and head on home. How they loved it. And for real pleasure, I would get out on the highways and back country roads back when they weren't so crowded and it was great fun to drive. Spun out a couple times on sharp curves, but didn't flip. Got rear-ended once, requiring repair and repainting. Engine overhaul at 250,000 miles. Dale Shoupe, my trusted mechanic, took lovingly good care of my Alfa, lubing and oiling and adjusting and minor repairs as needed.

I've never been a car guy. Never wanted to crawl under a car, struggling with wrenches while getting oil dripped on me. Hated washing, waxing and massaging the exterior. Wasn't interested in changing the plugs or adjusting the carburetor. My involvement under the hood was limited to the dipstick, adding oil or water when needed, or occasionally changing a flat tire. But I have always admired beauty and quality, and this Alfa Romeo model was so finely crafted and handsomely detailed that I continued to marvel at its elegant simplicity. It was instantly responsive, handled almost instinctively and embraced my body as if purposely designed to do so. And after a couple years I came to realize I had completely become one with this car.

So, on that sad, fateful Monday morning many years ago when I stepped out of the elevator into the underground garage of my Sixth Avenue apartment building and discovered my Alfa was not where I had left it the night before, I was bewildered, shocked and confused. I frantically looked all around among all the other cars but she was nowhere to be seen. My beloved Alfa was gone. <u>Gone</u>! And forlornly enveloped by this depressing reality, I dejectedly and hopelessly called the police.

Fortunately I had another car, an old Toyota Corolla, so I was able to get around. A couple days passed before I was able to deal with the finality of what had happened. I knew I needed to get another car. But what? How? All these years I had been faithful to my dear Alfa and paid no attention to other probably beautiful cars of high quality on the roadway. So now, by necessity, I began researching and casting about to discover something that would appeal to me, but without much luck.

On the third day, I was to meet my son Seth at our former home near the San Diego State University campus. As I left my apartment putting along in the old Toyota northward down Sixth Avenue to the 163 and then swinging east onto the I-8, my thoughts were swirling around my mind about important matters other than a new car. But as soon as I merged into traffic I glimpsed a car zipping along in the fast lane. It was a nice looking white car and its top was down but I couldn't tell its marque. So I decided to chase it and find out. But I just couldn't catch it. We passed Texas Street and were quickly approaching the Fairmount Avenue exit, which I would normally take to get to my old house. I decided to continue the pursuit. But I could not gain on that car. The next exit was College Avenue which could also get me to my house. Should I give up and leave the freeway? I decided not to quit and to keep up the chase. But alas, I couldn't get close enough and reluctantly decided to call it off and take the 70th Street exit. Then a quick right turn onto the west-bound frontage road parallel to and on the south side of the freeway.

Resigned to having missed a possibility I drove slowly back toward College Avenue, past Denny's, Marie Callender's and DZ Akins. The frontage road is separated from the freeway by a chain link fence, and as I'm driving along I notice something curious next to the fence. As I drew closer my heart leapt into my throat ......

.... There, right there, among all the cars parked along   the fence was ....

..... MY ALFA!

I was absolutely overwhelmed. I parked and did a cursory inspection. No damage, nothing missing. I unsteadily entered and took my rightful place behind the wheel. And sat there for the longest time, mulling over all the circumstances leading to this unlikely and stunning discovery.

First of all, I'm not a fatalist. I don't believe in predestination or karma or that things happen for a reason. By that I don't mean experiences that we deliberately plan and act on and choose to make happen. I think that the unplanned events that occur in our lives are the result of chance, coincidence, random intersections or accidental timing. Some call it blind luck, sometimes good, sometimes bad. So how else is it that I entered the freeway at that particular moment and was attracted by that particular car whizzing by just then. And that I couldn't catch it though I thought I could, and didn't take that first exit, or the second, and then instead of going on, chose to abandon my pursuit at the third exit, which in turn led me directly to my lost car. I mean what are the odds of all that happening the way it did, exponentially increasing at each step of the way? Astronomical! So I sat there, puzzled, and wondered... What's going on? What brought me here?

What I do know is that over the years I have left a lot of personal dust in this car. This Alfa Romeo has me written all over it. Is it possible that all this is the result of something other than chance? I don't think so .....

But.......??

LEN VEITZER
February 2014

A VISIT TO PARIS, PROVENCE AND THE HAUTE-LOIRE

I met Mary Duncan, a friend of Valerie Stallings who had brought her to Bread & Cie one Saturday morning in January, 2012. Mary is a writer and lives in San Diego and Paris. She is 72, grew up in National City, got her Master's and Doctorate and taught at San Diego State. She had recently published *"Henry Miller is Under My Bed,"* her memoir of *"People and Places on the Way to Paris."* She is short, chubby, smart and very strong-willed. She has lived in Paris about a dozen years but, surprisingly, has limited command of the language. She founded the *Paris Writers Group* and all of her considerable social life appears to be limited to English speaking friends.

She began to come frequently for coffee with the Saturday morning group at Bread & Cie, and then one day, knowing my interest in France, she invited me to visit her in Paris for a week in May. After rolling that around for half a second, I happily accepted. I had plenty of air miles with Delta and with no lodging expenses it would be a rare affordable opportunity. Then I thought that while there, why not go down to Provence in the South of France to visit old friends. When I told Mary of my plan, she suggested I also spend another week in Paris before returning to San Diego. Sounded good and so my planned excursion expanded to three engaging weeks in France.

Spending a week in Provence sounded exciting as well as economical. Judy Hawkins, my first friend in Aix-en-Provence in 1990, also lives in San Diego. She has an extra apartment in Aix and several times had offered me a stay there. When I called to accept, alas, her daughter will be there with her boyfriend at the same time and will be using the apartment. But Judy called our friend Lise Chevalier, an American married to Pierre, a Frenchman, and living in a small villa on the edge of the old city. Lise would be happy to host me for a few days. Wonderful!

Now for the last piece of the plan. My old dear, dear friend Caroline Chevalier (by coincidence, Pierre's first wife) no longer lives in Aix. About six years ago she bought a farm in the Haut-Loire area of mid-France. It had an old decrepit stone house on it, two stories with a caved-in roof. She spent two and a half years repairing, remodeling and transforming this old relic into a jewel. I wanted very much to visit her and so we emailed back and forth, setting up a three day visit on my way back to Paris after four days in Aix.

With 75,000 Delta miles, I bought a round trip coach ticket from San Diego to Paris, flying Delta to Atlanta on May 6th, changing to Air France and arriving in Paris around mid-day May 7th. My return would be on May 27th Paris to Atlanta to San Diego. I then bought online a one way $99 first class ticket on the TGV "bullet train" from Paris (Gare de Lyon) to Aix-en-Provence for May 14th. It's now March 22, 2012 and I'm counting down to the day I leave.

So six weeks later on May 6th I packed everything in one carry-on and my venerable brown sac-bag. They are stuffed full and are both heavy. Sheila came to pick me up at 11:30 and we got to the airport at noon. A brief and tender embrace and well wishes, and then into the terminal. It took a half hour to go through security, partly because my dopp kit with toilette items had to be examined separately. I then went to the gate and waited to talk to the attendant about upgrading but was told the plane is full. I then noticed that I had not retrieved my belt from the security tray. I had enough time to go back into the public area, go down the stairs to lost and found where I retrieved my belt. Then I had to go back through security. By the time I got back to the gate all passengers had boarded and there was no room in the overhead for my carry-on. It had to be checked through to CDG in Paris. I hate losing control of my luggage and hope it's there when I get there.

I had selected an aisle seat in the middle of the plane. I also brought a sandwich from home as well as some cheese and Italian salami. Sheila had packed some marinated shrimp and some pasta. I ate some on the plane and some in Atlanta. The trip from San Diego to Atlanta was easy and on time. I took the train to the international terminal for the Air France flight to Paris. Couldn't upgrade there either because I had bought my ticket with miles, not money. Waited around a couple hours and boarded. We were a half hour late leaving and consequently a half hour late getting to Paris (an 8 hour flight). The itinerary showed no meals on SD to ATL and only breakfast on Air France ATL to CDG. However when we left Atlanta at 11:30 p.m. they passed out menus for dinner. Late but welcome. Also terrible. Tried to sleep during the flight, but couldn't, feeling like a sardine in my tiny tin. Breakfast was pretty bad too. Then when I got to baggage claim at CDG, my suitcase never showed up. Mary had arranged to pick me up and luckily I found her waiting for me at the exit. I then went to Baggage Services to report and file a claim for my lost bag. They will look for it and if found, deliver it to Mary's apartment. In the meantime I have only the clothes I am wearing. If the loss is permanent I'm not sure yet what I will do. I then met Mary at the exit. She had her favorite cab driver with her and we drove back to her apartment.

It is located at 5, rue St. Romain, a block long street in a "desirable" area of the 6th Arrondisement, bordering the 7th. It is a small apartment with bedroom, bathroom, toilet room and kitchen. The living room is bright with large south facing windows, and has a dining table at one end and a small alcove with a day bed at the other where I slept. Mary takes great pride in the paint colors and furniture she selected, and indeed it looks very French and is an especially comfortable place.

I peeled off my clothes and took a much needed nap. Then Mary prepared a delicious salmon dinner, poured some good wine, and as we finished off the bottle, discussed our plans for the week. By now I'm feeling a little fatigued but think that after a good night's sleep tonight I'll be over any jet lag.

I slept fitfully till 7:30, then up for an hour and back down for a "brief" nap. Mary had called Air France about the lost luggage – it was found and would be delivered between 10 and 2. It was 11:00 when I woke again from a knock on the front door – my suitcase was delivered, intact. Mary and I went out to buy a couple of *pains chocolat* (a delicious squarish puff pastry similar to a croissant and riddled with chocolate in the center). She showed me around the neighborhood and we returned to eat our breakfast pastries. Hung out for the afternoon, talking and exploring possible tours to the Loire Valley. No decisions. At 7:30 we walked a half block to the little brasserie *Landais* for dinner.

I had roast pork, which was tasty but tough. We shared a pichet of wine. Then back at the apartment I continued to explore tours on Mary's computer while she was finishing a book she was reading. I went to bed at 11:00, woke at 2:00 and could not go back to sleep until 5:00! Awful night.

I awoke refreshed at 8:30 Wednesday morning. Mary had coffee ready and had prepared muesli for breakfast. We went over plans for the day, watched the news, etc. Around 11:00 we took the Metro to the Latin Quarter along the Seine. Later we visited *Shakespeare and Co.*, an English language bookstore, where Mary has a lot of history. The shop

is crammed everywhere with books, mostly used, and periodicals. A place with a glorious literary history. Shelves on every possible surface and books on every possible shelf. There are also more books upstairs as well as a small reading area and an alcove where itinerant literary types, hard pressed for cash, could stay for the night.

Indeed, Mary had been a "guest" when she first arrived in Paris. Today she inquired about how her book was selling – fairly well, she was told.

We left to walk on *rue de la Boucherie* where Mary pointed out World War 2 places and historical events. She identified the houses of the two 16-year old Jewish boys who were rounded up from their school on July 16, 1942 together with several thousand others from all of France, all of whom were shipped to concentration camps. She is writing a book about these boys, one of whom escaped, is still living, and is an important resource.

We then walked a couple blocks for Mary's 12:30 lunch reservation at one of her favorite restaurants, *Bistro Le Reminet*. It is the kind of local restaurant one thinks of as typically French, small, with excellent service and offering a fine menu. I had salad with chicken livers and then baked cod and potatoes. We skipped dessert.

We returned to the apartment on the Metro, rested, and prepared

for the evening. Our evening plan was to attend the annual meeting of the AARO (Association of American Residents Overseas) with financial reports, new Board of Directors, etc. They are mostly conservatives concerned about U.S. and French taxes and preserving their wealth. After an hour the meeting adjourned for cocktails and hors d'ouvres, which were the most imaginative and delicious I'd ever had. Then back to the apartment. It was about 11:00 and we were getting very tired and Mary went right to bed. I stayed up for a little while longer before hitting the daybed but awoke at 1:30 and couldn't go back to sleep. I finally did manage and slept until 8:30.

Mary always makes coffee in the morning, which was hot and particularly welcome today because outside it was cold and drizzling when we went out to buy some *pains chocolat*. We came back, ate the *pains*, and prepared to go to the *Musee Rodin*, a couple of Metro stops away. Mary had made (forged) press passes, so we went right in, no lines, no fees. The Rodins were magnificent, mostly bronze sculptures, some in marble, and many drawings and paintings.

After dinner we changed clothes, went back to the Metro and on to the *Village Voice Bookshop* on rue Princesse in the heart of Saint-Germain-des-Prés for a symposium on Lawrence Durell, poet and author of many novels (including *The Alexandria Quartet*), close friend

of Henry Miller, Anais Nin and other literary giants of the '50s and '60s. The shelves and tables were overflowing with English language books, journals and rare magazines. Up a narrow spiral staircase to an open, low-ceilinged room were the four participants seated in a cluster, and for those in attendance the seating in tiny chairs was tight and crowded. I'm particularly interested in Durell because I'm just finishing the fourth book of his Quartet. Among the attendees were a few English speakers but most were French. And the presentations and the subsequent dialogues were all in French. So there was not much for me to appreciate. Then all adjourned to a small cinema a few blocks away to see two short films on Durrell.

One was entirely in French and the other about half and half. For me it was not worth the 11 Euros. We returned to the apartment and I was totally spent. I crawled wearily into my daybed, and with a great sigh of exhaustion, fell quickly asleep. And except for the few usual trips to the bathroom, I got a full restoring night's sleep.

It was Friday morning and I was up by 7:30, washed and shaved, and went out to the boulangerie to buy a couple of *pains chocolat* and a *demi-baguette* (1/2). The *pains* were delicious as usual, light and flaky with small chunks of chocolate throughout. The *baguette* was a disappointment – the crust was soft, not at all crunchy.

There was a light rain falling so it seemed like a good day to go to a museum – namely the *D'Orsay*. We got there about noon and breezed

in with our press passes. There is so much to see and not enough time for all. And it was crowded. So we decided to limit our viewing, starting with a new exhibit, several rooms filled with Degas nudes. His early pencil sketches while in training are breathtaking. I've always appreciated his work but not to the extent I do now. After about an hour with Degas we went up to the 5th floor and the Impressionists. I had seen these in 1990 when I last visited Paris. Then again two summers ago at the *DeYoung Museum* in San Francisco with my son Jason and his wife Jane where many pieces were loaned by the *D'Orsay* in two increments (spring and fall). But for me, I can't get too much of the Impressionists. By 3:00 I was very tired and my legs were aching terribly. It was just past time for some lunch and we stopped at a small restaurant a couple blocks from the museum, "*Le 20 Bellechasse.*" It looked good but it all turned out to be a most unmemorable lunch.

Back to the Metro and the apartment by 4:00 and I crashed for a restorative hour. Unfortunately, this morning I began to feel maybe a cold coming on (runny nose). I'm doing what I can to stave it off. Mary went out to do some shopping and bought some soup – puree of vegetable to which she shredded some fresh basil from a pot on her window sill. My cold is developing – <u>not good!</u> Went to bed about 10:00. Spent a horrible night. Couldn't sleep because my sinuses were draining, I was coughing and nose blowing. However, gratefully no sore throat, headache or upset stomach. Finally slept from 3:00 to 8:00.

Woke the next day with a stuffy blowy nose. Looks like a nice day but I decided to stay in to treat this stupid cold. We had hoped to go to the Tuilleries today, but now that's iffy. Mary went out and bought a couple of our usual *pains chocolat* for breakfast. I needed to go to the "Orange" electronics store three blocks away to buy a European SIM card for my mobile phone. The clerk installed the card in my phone but they didn't have a 25 Euro plan and I had to go to a *tabac* across the street for that. Then I stopped at a *pharmacie* to buy some more Sudafed. Back to the apartment to take it easy, do some reading and conserve my energy. Mary went out shopping and got some lamb chops for dinner as well as some cheese. A little later we ate dinner, after which we watched a movie on Mary's I-Pad (*A Room With a View*). Good movie, but watching on an I-Pad sucks. Went to bed at 12:30 and slept the whole night through. Best night since I've been here.

Woke at 7:30 on this bright and sunny morning feeling fully rested for a change. We had coffee and shared a *tarte*. Using Mary's computer, I vainly tried to find an earlier connection in Atlanta for San

Diego to avoid the 4-1/2 hour layover. We watched some news and had a good conversation about things Parisian. About noon we went out and took the #39 bus right down to the *Tuilleries* at the edge of the immense courtyard of the Louvre.

We passed under the massive arch and walked the length of the Gardens (about a half-mile) observing other strollers and families enjoying a crisp sunny Sunday in this great civic treasure. All over the gardens on both sides of the central promenade are large bronze sculptures, many by Maillol. It's a remarkable and enviable example of public art, especially in such a pastoral setting.

After we returned to the central courtyard of the Louvre, we went down through the iconic Pyramid to the Apple store where Mary wanted to resolve some issues with her I-Pad. Then the #39 bus to rue St. Germaine and lunch at "Le Bonaparte."

Le Bonaparte

Finally the #39 again back to the apartment. I was tired, changed my clothes and flopped down for two hours till 6:00.

Mary was getting ready to go to small gathering of friends for a talk about Simone de Beauvoire. I was disinvited because Mary thought my coughing and sniffling could be worrisome to the others. That was fine with me. It gave me time to prepare for tomorrow's ride on the TGV to Aix. When she returned, I asked Mary to arrange for M. Mattos, her favorite taxi driver, to pick me up tomorrow morning at 11:30 to take me to the Gare de Lyon. I packed, showered and ate some cheese, olives and bread. I'm excited about being in Aix tomorrow.

It was Monday May 12th. I had slept well and awoke feeling much better. Mary prepared coffee and breakfast, we watched the news and talked about her coming week. M. Mattos and his taxi were waiting for me at 11:30 to take me to the Gare de Lyon. Though I had enough time, I had trouble finding the right car. But I did with two minutes to spare and settled into my first class single seat, albeit facing backwards. The train left on time, as it always does. The TGV raced swiftly and silently as it passed through the beautiful countryside of farms and meadows, sometimes with grazing cattle or sheep. This train did not stop in Lyon but continued through to the new station just outside of Aix-en-Provence, three hours after leaving Paris.

Lise was to pick me up but she wasn't there. After 10 or 15 minutes I called her on her mobile. She had been there, but I apparently had waited on the wrong side of the station. She returned, picked me up and we arrived at her house, "L'Ombreuse" about 3:00 o'clock. She

showed me to a lovely guest room with a view of beautiful roses and the garden beyond.

I changed my clothes and joined Lise on the patio overlooking a verdant back yard with grass, trees and so many flowers. We talked at length about how things had changed in Aix, what things hadn't, and of the friends I once knew. Soon Pierre arrived and poured some *pastis* for the three of us. It was all so calm and temporal, birds chirping, a mild breeze and congenial conversation. Pierre appeared not to have changed much, still with a reddish beard and mustache and serious demean-or. He retired from Shell Oil about 15 years ago and busies himself with projects around the house as well as for a daughter who lives in Marseilles. He also has nine cars and four motorcycles to tend to. Lise is active in the community, has become a little dour, and has visually aged since I last saw her ten years ago I also sense a slight degree of impatience and discontent.

When it turned cool on the patio, Lise and I went inside while Pierre decided to mow the grass. He then joined us for more *pastis* and conversation. We enjoyed a late dinner --- Lise had prepared a delicious shrimp and rice meal and finished off with a very tasty peach *tarte*. It had been a busy and scintillating day and by 11:00 o'clock I was spent and went to bed. I must have been really tired because I slept till 10:00.

Lise brewed a pot of most welcome coffee and cut some delicious melon as well. We watched the Hollande inauguration, impressively

just 11 days after the election. We in the U.S. are used to two and a half months, with a lame duck president and many congressmen, before government can begin to function again. Lise drove me into town and dropped me off at Le Rotunde with its large and majestic ornate fountain. I leisurely walked my favorite boulevard, the familiar Cours Mirabeau, like a prodigal son. The open air markets in the several *Places* (plazas) were closing and cleaning up.

I learned also that my dear friends, the elderly Maurice and Denise Berne, had both passed away several years earlier. I was not surprised but it still was a shock.

I paused and reminisced at the forbidding doorway of the Hotel Particulaire which I had discovered on my first trip to Aix in October of 1989, and where I had stayed for a week and a half.

And I wandered over to the Restaurant Shalimar, a small friendly neighborhood cafe which I loved and where I dined about once a week. It was gone and replaced with a wine bar.

Le Jardin de Luculu, a favorite of mine run by two dedicated women and renowned for their desserts and gracious hospitality, was gone and replaced with a pizza joint.

I returned to the Cours Mirabeau and settled in at a small outdoor table at Le Grillon, also a restaurant I frequently enjoyed. Right in front, in the middle of the Cours is the 2,000 year old moss-covered Roman fountain, still flowing and a convenient respite for thirsty pedestrians.

At 2:30 I nursed a *pastis*, contentedly watching the parade of so many people on the broad sidewalk in front of me. Shoppers, businessmen, school children and strikingly beautiful high-heeled women slowly promenading.

I ordered lunch -- a sandwich of chevre and tapenade, and watched an ongoing variety of buskers and street entertainers.

I was a little concerned about my legs managing the half mile walk back to L'Ombreuse. But at 3 o'clock I walked and I was okay, then changed my clothes and rested for an hour. We watched a press conference with Angela Merkel after which Pierre arrived and we all shared a great salad that Lise had prepared. Like any decent French meal we were un-hurried, savoring our salad, our splendid wine and dessert and fine bread and a quartet of cheeses. And then, finally, after a full day, to bed at 10:30.

my top floor windows at 15, rue Merindol

When I awoke at 6 o'clock and realized nobody else was up and there was nothing I needed to do, I went back to sleep and rose at 9:00. Lise was up and had already had breakfast but she prepared a chilled bowl of fresh fruit for me, and with a bracing cup of coffee I was ready to launch my day.

It was a cool, partly cloudy day as I walked to the Gare and bought a first class ticket to Le Puy to visit Caroline on the 18th. It would be a two leg trip with the TGV north to Lyon, then transferring to a local train southwest to Le Puy.

I continued on to visit my old neighborhood and lingered at 15, rue Merindol. Everything appeared unchanged from when I left it 22 years

earlier. I sat down across the narrow street and reflected for a long while about how it was then and how much I had loved my extraordinary top floor apartment and the fulfilling year of happy times I spent there.

The entrance to
15, rue Merindol

A block away was a small *Place* that a couple of restaurants shared for outdoor dining during good weather. I used to frequent one of them just steps away from my home. Of course it was gone, but was replaced by a new café, *Angelina*. I enjoyed a lovely lunch as I reminisced about the many occasions spent in this quiet, intimate *Place* right there in my old neighborhood.

I did a little shopping because I wanted to buy a scarf for Sheila, but most stores were closed. So I ambled over to Le Grillon for a café. Later I resumed shopping but found nothing I thought she would like. I trudged back to L'Ombreuse. Lise had gone out to pick up a friend at the TGV station, so I found a beer in the fridge which I heartily enjoyed as I sat out in the patio recounting my nostalgic day. But I still had that nuisance of a chest congestion that wore me out so I went down for an hour's nap about 5:15.

Lise had returned with her friend Connie and they were chatting away in the kitchen. We all settled in the living room as I joined the conversation. Connie is about 40, a writer from Berkeley who had come again to Aix for a week-long conference with "Zona Rosa," a writers' group that also includes Lise. After a bit, Pierre, who had been repairing the bathroom in his daughter's apartment in Marseilles, returned home, and fortified with generous dollops of *pastis*, we all sat and watched the news. A little later, Judy Hawkins called and advised that the AAGP (Anglo American Group of Provence) would be meeting tomorrow at *Bar Darius* instead of its usual place. I wanted to continue shopping for Sheila but because tomorrow is a holiday, all the stores would be closed. Lise suggested *Zara* (a fashionable shop) for a scarf, maybe Friday morning.

I woke at 8:00, showered and joined Lise and Connie for a little breakfast. Lise's long time friend Nancy and Nancy's niece Amy came over and we all walked to the *Bar Darius* to meet with the AAGP for coffee. I had been an active member, formed many friendships, and

engaged in countless interesting and informative activities when I lived here. Today I met a lively congenial group, but not surprisingly after so many years, did not include anyone I knew.

As we left we noticed that the *Zara* store was open. I

browsed for an appropriate scarf but found nothing to my liking. We all continued on to the nearby parking lot where Lise had parked and we all piled into her car.

We drove south for half an hour to La Ciotat, a small village at the Mediterranean seashore. We stopped first for cocktails and hors d'ouvres at the home of a British couple, Uta and Robert, and then we all walked together to the heart of the village. A lovely and charming place, arcing beautifully around a tranquil bay with a variety of many boats tied up along the shore.

We all filed in to *L'Escalet*, Lise's favorite waterfront restaurant, where the congenial *propriataire* seated us at a large table. We engaged in lively and animated conversation as we ate heartily and drank copiously of the local wine. An excellent typically French two-hour lunch. We split the check, 30 Euros each including wine and comp for Lise.

As we were settling the bill the very thoughtful *proprietaire* cut up some steak for Uta's dog, earning himself her thanks together with a very nice tip.

After lunch we walked all the way to the far end of the very picturesque harbor and back before returning to Uta and Robert's house. We then drove up the narrow, steep winding road to the crest of the "mountain" behind the village, which afforded us with spectacular views of *La Ciotat* and the adjacent town of *Cassis* and their harbors. On the way back to Aix we dropped off Nancy and Amy and were back to L'Ombreuse by 6:00. I rested for a half hour before a light, simple supper with Lise and Connie. It was about 10:30 when I faded out, appreciating what had been a good full day.

My chest congestion and coughing is seriously slowing me down and I longingly miss Sheila. I thought about maybe leaving France early.

I slept very well till 5:30, but since no one else was stirring, I languished in bed until 7:30, thinking about today's journey to visit Caroline. It had been a rainy night. It was still drizzly out, and cold. Lise had prepared a bowl of fresh fruit and coffee, after which I returned to my room and packed. I needed to buy some Euros so Lise dropped me off near the BNP bank where I used my new (temporary) Bank of America debit card to exchange for 100 Euros. It was about 9:30 so I decided not to continue shopping for a scarf because stores had not yet opened. It had stopped raining but it was still cold as I walked back to L'Ombreuse. Connie was up and we had toast and more coffee as she described her life in Berkeley and what she wanted to accomplish during her week here with the writers group.

Then I had to leave, as I was going take the shuttle bus to the TGV Gare. But Lise returned from her errands and offered to drive me to the Gare. I thanked her warmly for being such a thoughtful and generous host. Arriving at the Gare an hour early I bought a tuna sandwich that was so bad I threw it away and bought a brownie instead.

As I sat, waiting and munching, I thought back on the last few days and my reconnection with this place I loved. Then the strangest, unexpected sensation settled over me. All the friends I knew 22 years ago, except for Lise and Judy, are gone. The places that so filled me with joy in this city are both changed and unchanged. My only imprint is in my own memory. I suppose the reality so hard to recognize at the time was that I was just passing through. My footprints are long gone. And although my memories, precious as they are, still linger, I look back on these last few days as the unexpected closing of a book. I do so with nostalgia and smiles, but also with finality. I will probably never return.

I soon boarded and easily found the proper car and seat, and the journey northward to Lyon was swift and comfortable. There I had a two hour layover before transferring to the local train heading southwesterly to Le Puy. I tried calling Sheila but this phone doesn't seem to work to the U.S.

I boarded and found my first class seat. There were many stops along the way as we rose through beautiful, densely forested, rugged

mountains. At Firminy the electric overhead lines ended and the engine was changed from electric to diesel. We needed to stop in Veley to wait for an opposing train since there is only one track into Le Puy. I called Caroline about the delay, and the train finally arrived in Le Puy at 8:00, an hour late. She was there patiently waiting, visibly older but with her hair typically frazzled and her bright blue eyes twinkling mischievously as I remember her. We embraced warmly and gazed so lovingly at each other. We piled into her new bright red Renault and drove for half an hour to her house.

Le Puy is at an elevation of 600 meters (about 2,000 ft) and she lives 25 km away at 1,200 meters. The road is long and winding, much of it a single lane, through beautiful countryside, forests and farms. We finally arrive at her two-story stone house, solitarily set on 10,000 sq. meters (2½ acres). We are in a lush plain with farms, cattle and sheep ranches high up in the Haut-Loire area of mid-France. It is cold and windy.

Caroline showed me the entire house, a rectangular two-story stone structure built about 150 years ago. It was vacant and in total disrepair when she bought it five years earlier. The roof was caved in, half the second floor was missing, as were the windows and doors. She spent two and a half years rehabilitating it with a talented local architect and a competent contractor. They turned it into a jewel of a home.

At one end of the ground floor was a large room that had been used for hay storage as well as a haven for a few head of cattle during heavy weather. It became a perfect studio for Caroline and her ceramic work.

Also on the ground floor was an open kitchen and dining room separated from the living room beyond by a two-way fireplace. In one corner of the living room was a small alcove where Caroline sleeps, and an adjacent small bath-room.

All these rooms have large windows and doors opening to the distant views. Three spacious bed-rooms are up-stairs as well as a footed tub in a large bathroom, and a separate toilet room.

All the bedrooms are tastefully furnished and one has a classic pool/billiards table.

Caroline showed me to one of the other bedrooms which was to be "my room," and I unloaded all my stuff.

Extensive windows grace the bedrooms too, allowing light, ventilation and the same spectacular views.

I met her dog Perli, I think the ugliest dog I've ever seen. Caroline thinks he's part Husky and I think part wolf or dingo. He is about five years old, medium size, medium nose, short hair of mottled gray with brown splotches, which looks like camouflage. Caroline broke up laughing when I called Perli an "army dog." He doesn't bark and must have been terribly abused as a puppy because he's very fearful and suspicious, and jumps away with his tail between his legs at one's slightest movement. But we quickly became friends.

Caroline poured some wine (from a box) as she cooked dinner, and we talked at great length about our children and grand-children. And more conversation about French politics. She doesn't like Sarkozy at all and she is thrilled that Hollande was elected president. Then, after this long day, to bed in our respective rooms.

I must have been particularly weary from yesterday's arduous hustle and bustle because I slept till 9:00 o'clock. After washing up I tried to shave but my electric shaver cord didn't fit any of the new outlets so I will go without shaving for three days. We had a leisurely breakfast of fruit, toast and coffee and talked about our children and their lives. My lung congestion and stuffy nose continue unabated, leading to annoying discomfort and frustration. My handkerchiefs were all filled and needed attention, so I took a few minutes to wash them thoroughly and hang them outside to dry.

Every day Caroline takes Perli out for a run. So we hop in her car and go for a slow drive along the narrow country roads while Perli races ahead of us. He tires after a kilometer or so, clambers back in the car and we drive back home. Caroline is soon in her garden diligently planting more flowers. Later she begins preparing a lamb stew for lunch. It was well seasoned and full of flavor, and of course was accompanied by a glass of local wine. She then informed me that we are going to a concert tonight. Then, on Caroline's computer I made train reservations from Le Puy (local train) to St. Etienne and then to Paris (TGV) for Monday May 21. First class was filled so I had to settle for second class. I was ready for a nap so I went upstairs, flopped for two hours and changed clothes.

We left at 4:15 for the concert at a small, very old stone church in Moudeyres, a half hour drive on one lane, sometimes dirt, roads. It is like the many small towns on this broad verdant plain, 2-3 miles apart and with about 300 to 400 inhabitants. The towns also serve the needs of the many adjacent farmers and ranchers. At the church there were about 35 music lovers seated on old wooden pews. I selected the front row to best observe and listen to a duet of modern music, part of a series of concerts at this church. The one hour program featured a

French woman on the harpsichord and a lovely Japanese woman in a beautiful kimono singing and plucking three stringed instruments. It was such a beautiful and exquisite performance.

On the way back we stopped at *Bar Les Cevennes*, a Caroline hangout, for a drink. She introduced me to her close friend the bartender, 30ish, a wisp of a woman and with a warm open smile. Perli played outside and was soon joined by two more dogs, uglier even than him. Maybe it's the water.

There were about a half dozen customers scattered about the small room. The walls were adorned with a mélange of artwork by local artists, all for sale. We stayed for about an hour.

On the way back Caroline toured me around the hills past old castles and small villages. The air is clear and clean. The views are spectacular with broad meadows of grazing cows, sheep and horses, forests of deciduous and evergreen in many shades of green.

When we got back to the house around 8 o'clock it was still light outside and cold and very windy, but no rain. Caroline fixed dinner – a pot of mussels, salad and cheese and more wine. We talked for a long while and as it was now close to 10:00, I went to bed but I couldn't sleep. It was an erratic night.

I awoke at 8:00 on this cold and rainy Sunday morning. But it took an hour to get up, as I lay in this warm bed contemplating cutting my stay in Paris short and leaving early. I decided to stick it out (for now).

Caroline had been up for a couple hours but thoughtfully prepared coffee and toast for me. I had time then to take photos, but as it was too nasty to go outside I concentrated only on the interiors. For almost two weeks I've been in a news vacuum so I was able to use Caroline's computer to log onto the internet and filled myself with the New York Times, the L.A. Times and (yuk) the San Diego Union-Tribune.

Caroline suggested we go upstairs and shoot some pool. She's a talented player and we both enjoyed the play. We split two games of 8-ball and then she taught me how to play French billiards, which is difficult and takes much skill. It was good fun. Through it all, I'm still plagued with my chest congestion, frequent coughing and stuffy nose. It is a continual frustration.

For lunch Caroline prepared the day's major meal, a delicious variety of tomatoes, peas, potatoes, duck, strawberries, cheese and coffee, and of course, wine. We spent the afternoon indoors as it was still raining and I may not get any exterior photos. I tried my cell phone to the U.S. but with no luck, as Caroline played a solitaire game with big marbles. As she was cooking I had a bourbon cocktail before sitting down to dinner. Later, on the internet, I looked into Paris weather for the coming week --- rain on Monday and Tuesday, partly cloudy Wednesday and sunny Thursday and Friday. We talked more about French and American politics and she is very hopeful for Obama. At 9:30 it was still light outside but I went to bed at 10:00.

I arose at 7:30 on my last morning in this idyllic mountain area. Many thoughts filled my consciousness as I packed my few belongings. I went down for a quiet breakfast as if we both knew it might be our last. It was foggy and raining out, seeming to punctuate our anxiety. I said goodbye to Perli and we left for Le Puy at 8:45, arriving at the Gare at 9:30. As the train wasn't leaving till 10:30 we went across the street, in the rain, to a bar for café and croissants.

Then back at the Gare and tearful farewells and lingering looks, both knowing that this is probably the last time we will ever see each other. I was very introspective on the ride to St. Ettienne as I tenderly recalled the many warm and loving times we had together. She is an important part of my history and I'm so very thankful to have had her in my life.

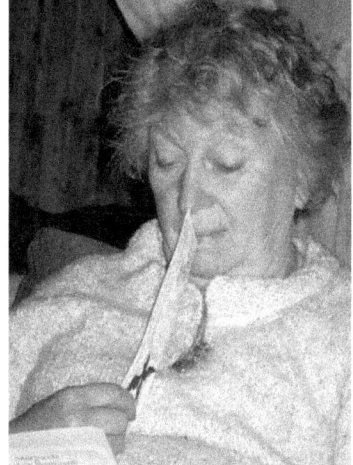

203

At St. Ettienne I changed trains to the TGV to Paris with a stop in Lyon. I took a better seat, but when many new passengers boarded at Lyon I had to return to my assigned seat (again sitting backwards) behind a mother and baby. When the train left at 1:10 the baby started crying and wailed the entire two hours to Paris. I installed earplugs I had brought and they helped a little. Rolling into Paris through the suburbs the view of graffiti everywhere on walls, vehicles and any available surface was ugly and depressing. We arrived at Gare de Lyon in Paris at mid-afternoon and it was still raining when I went out and waited in the queue for a taxi. The GPS guided trip to Mary's was swift and efficient and cost 11.1 Euros. Mary was very happy to see me and I was glad to be back, in spite of my incessant coughing and sinus. So I changed clothes, poured a scotch, relaxed and shared some of my experiences with Mary, then later unpacked.

Today is Sheila's birthday so I called her from the bathroom (for privacy) with my new-found method (001-619-435-1188) to wish her a happy birthday. She was surprised and delighted to hear from me. She's going to L.A. for a couple days for a doctor's appointment and to visit her daughter.

Mary and I watched some news and she prepared a delicious dinner – roast chicken, very tasty, and green beans. We decided to watch a movie (Goodfellas) and after this long and exhausting day I finally hit the daybed for the night. At 6 a.m. I was awakened by the upstairs TV or radio but managed to sleep another hour.

It's a cool and cloudy day today. I went out for *pains chocolat* and a *demi-baguette* as Mary slept till 9:00. She prepared coffee and we began to make plans for the day. We left about 11:00 and walked three blocks to *Le Bon Marche*, a high-end department store, something like Nordstroms. Still shopping, I was excited to find a scarf for Sheila at 95 Euros, colorful, beautiful and just right. We then walked to the Musee Maillol that had many paintings by 17th century artists, but only a few of Maillol's sculptures and some of his paintings, all nudes. Generally boring and disappointing.

From there we walked through the Latin Quarter to *Salon du The* for lunch. We each chose dorado, which was presented as a whole fish, together with rice, and was absolutely delicious. We took the Metro back and I must have been really spent because I napped from 3:30 to 5:00. Later Mary's friend Ron came over with his assistant

Rhowan to plan some repairs to the apartment while I searched on her computer for an excursion to Versailles. But with no good results and feeling lousy I decided to forego Versailles.

My chest congestion and coughing are relentless. Mary was worried about pneumonia and suggested I see a doctor here in Paris, but I didn't want to start any kind of treatment here since I'd be leaving soon. She then suggested I call my doctor in San Diego, a pretty good idea. And I miss Sheila terribly. I'm thinking seriously about returning to San Diego three days early on Thursday, pay the $250 penalty (which I would have spent here anyway) so I can see Dr. Price on Friday. But I'll sleep on it tonight.

Originally scheduled to leave on Sunday, I did decide to change my return to tomorrow morning, Thursday May 24th, and I spent two hours making the change with Delta/Air France. I was able to select the flights I wanted, namely Air France non-stop to L.A. in 10 hours and 40 minutes leaving at 10:30, and also because the French food is so good. Then SkyWest, a commuter flight arriving in San Diego at 4:09 in the afternoon.

I called Sheila to give her the info while Mary went to the bank and also to the *boulangerie* for *pains chocolat*. Around mid-day we took the Metro across the Seine to the Right Bank and walked a few blocks

to "Inn Christ Bistro," a small restaurant recommended to Mary by a friend. It was just so-so.

We had then planned a boat ride on the Seine but there wasn't much time and I was dragging, so we came back to the apartment and I rested for an hour.

We left at 5:20 for the American University of Paris for a lecture by the iconic historian David McCullough, winner of Pulitzers for *"John Adams"* and *"Harry Truman,"* about his new book *"The Greater Journey: Americans in Paris."* A very good read, interesting and informative. We arrived early and found "reserved" tags on all the chairs. When we asked for clarification, we were told to sit anywhere. And we did, in the second row. Mary had earlier assumed that the appropriate attire would be "Paris casual" and we dressed accordingly. Then people started arriving and were dressed much differently, men in suits and ties, women in lovely outfits. But we didn't much care.

McCullough was there as part of the celebration of the University's  50th anniversary, and to be the Commencement Speaker the next day. He spoke tonight for an hour and a half about the Americans who journeyed to Paris in the 19th Century (1830-1895) and about how they returned to America with experiences and insights that profoundly helped shape the evolving American culture. What an excellent talk augmented with many archival photographs. We enjoyed snacks afterward in an adjacent room prior to returning to the apartment.

I called Dr. Price and left a message request to Myrene for an urgent appointment any time on Friday and to call my home phone and leave a message for the time. I then called Sheila to clarify the pick-up place (Commuter Terminal). She wants to cook dinner. I said thank you, but no, I will take you out to dinner.

Went to bed at 10:00 with happy anticipation, awoke at 4:00, slept some more and rose at 6:30.

After washing and shaving, I finished packing as Mary made coffee. I offered my heartfelt thanks and gratitude as we said our goodbyes and I hustled my baggage down the steep stairway to the street. M. Mattos was waiting with his taxi to take me to the airport, a 40 minute drive through morning traffic. I'm so very grateful to Mary for the rare opportunity to have come to visit Paris. She is a wonderful host, considerate and generous, and I owe her my deeply felt gratitude.

Uncertain if I was in the right concourse at CDG, I did manage to find my way to security. They were very thorough and efficient and frisked me from head to foot. I found my way to Gate 46 by 9:00 with boarding to start at 9:45. I boarded and settled into my aisle seat about mid-plane again in the sardine section. Scheduled to leave at 10:30 we left a half-hour late. At 12:00 I ate the ham sandwich Mary had made for me. Then a lunch was served at 1:00 of Lebanese-style bulgur wheat salad, Basque-style chicken, wheat berries with vegetables and a vanilla éclair. It all sounded so delicious, yet was atrocious and inedible. But the wine was good and particularly welcome.

What a long and arduous trip. After what seemed like six hours I glanced at my watch and couldn't believe only three hours had passed. I walked around frequently for relief from my cramped quarters, tried to doze but couldn't, and read a little.

A couple hours before landing in L.A. dinner was served. Vegetable salad, smoke-dried chicken and Sardinian-style potato salad all looked so good on the menu, but unbelievably, was worse than lunch. The cheese was so-so, the chocolate cake was disappointing, but again, the wine was good. And I had taken such pains to book Air France because of the great cuisine. *Quelle dommage*.

We landed a half hour late at LAX and it took close to an hour to get through immigration and customs. In order to get to my connecting AirWest flight to San Diego I had to leave the terminal, board a shuttle to a different terminal and bear the nuisance of going through security again. The quick flight arrived at the Commuter Terminal in San Diego on time at 4:10. I picked up my luggage on the tarmac, walked through the terminal and happily spotted Sheila with her car waiting at the curb. A truly joyous greeting, then out to dinner and finally, to my house.

RECAP AND REFLECTION

Although I had no particular or romantic feelings for Mary, I accepted her invitation because she was a good friend and it was a good opportunity to visit Paris, having last been there once in 1990.

And she was a most thoughtful, considerate and generous host. Unfortunately my illness plagued me the entire trip – fatigue, aches, incessant hacking and general malaise precluded my visiting so many places I wanted to experience in Paris. But together with air mileage and friends' hosting it was all very affordable.

Although my visit to Aix was brief, it was long enough. Fulfilling, but surprisingly bittersweet at best.

Caroline is still perky and endearing, but she has aged considerably since I last saw her ten years earlier, and I suppose her reaction to me must have been the same. My visit with her was particularly enjoyable but not as well engaged as it would have been had I been healthier and not contagious. So in spite of our delicious history I did not advance any intimacy while at her house. I was not feeling at all well and had so little energy. Yet I will probably never see her again and should have paid more attention to the approaching finality.

I'm sorry I didn't have more of a chance to savor French cuisine and local wine in small restaurants. Because staying with hosts tends to lend itself to "home cooking."

EPILOG

By the end of the year Sheila and I both recognized that we had less in common than we originally had thought and that our differences had become more apparent. We sadly acknowledged that the magic and excitement that exploded last spring had slowly disappeared, and we agreed to fondly remember those best of times, remain good friends, but go our separate ways.

LEN VEITZER
January 2015

GREENWOOD

During breaks from my architectural studies at U.C. Berkeley I would find temporary employment with architects in San Diego. I had become an excellent draftsman -- fast, accurate and thorough, and I could easily find a job. One summer in the mid-'50s I began working for Bob Bradt in his downtown office. Bob was a fine and capable architect, and although he would occasionally design houses, he primarily specialized in commercial, municipal and institutional buildings. And my role would be to translate his designs into construction drawings.

It was a good job where I was able to gain useful experience in a congenial environment with Bob and another draftsman, as well as being able to salt away a few bucks for my next year at the university. I eventually received my degree in architecture, got my license, opened an office and gradually built an active practice. At the same time my wife Nadene and I joyfully filled our lives with five fine children. It was a challenging but altogether a happy time.

But many years later, after a two year battle with cancer, my brave and stoic mother died. My father had hated the prospect of being buried in a hole in the ground so he long ago purchased adjoining crypts in the Jewish Mausoleum in the only San Diego cemetery that had a Jewish section, located at 43rd and Imperial Avenue in Southeast San Diego.

It was such a sad day. So many mourners had already entered the building as many others were continually arriving. It was the middle of the day in the middle of August and although the sky was overcast it was still hot and uncomfortably humid. As our family alighted from our limos and slowly walked toward the entrance, I glanced up at the mausoleum and was suddenly enveloped by a bewildering sensation. It was not at all connected with the grief I was struggling with but was nevertheless unsettling and strange and confusing.

I had this growing and soon overwhelming sense that I had experienced this before.

Soon after entering through the front doors I looked to the left -- and mysteriously knew what I would see. Yes, there it was, a long, wide corridor flanked with marble-faced crypts that rose from the floor to the high ceiling. And I just knew I would see the same when I looked to the right. Straight ahead, amid the subdued murmurs of the many guests, was a large area with rows of chairs facing a lectern and the coffin bedecked with chrysanthemums, and beyond that through flanking windows, as I was certain, was the view of a lush and pastoral garden. How could I know this. My head was spinning and this was getting a little spooky. I don't remember ever having been here before. What was going on here?

THEN LIKE A BOLT IT HIT ME!

Yes, I HAD been here before! At the drafting table that summer 25 years ago in Bob Bradt's office when I had drawn all the construction drawings, the blueprints, for this building.

When I returned four years later when my father died, I completed the connection begun a long time ago, back to the Greenwood Mausoleum, where I had been *twice* before.

LEN VEITZER
August 2014

CARNEVALE

Three months prior to my moving to France I had journeyed to the South of France to discover the area where I wanted to live. When I arrived in Aix-en-Provence I instinctively knew that this was the place and then set about to explore and to meet new friends, both French and expat Americans. Among them was Judy Hawkins, who was very helpful in orienting me to the old city. She is from California and has lived in Aix for eight years. She is married and her husband lives and works in Denver. They see each other three or four times a year. Judy was about 40, a short haired brunette of medium height and with a narrow face. She had an open and outgoing personality and loved to talk in her rapid fire way of speaking. She also helps new arrivals seek housing, which I of course would need.

A few weeks after I returned to San Diego, deeply involved in planning and organizing my move, I got a phone call from Judy. Her friend Lili, an American from California, lives in Aix and will be gone for two weeks about the time I would be arriving, and her apartment would be available to me to rent while I'm looking for a place of my own. I called Lili the next day and we made all the arrangements. Things were beginning to fall into place and this just intensified my level of excitement and anticipation.

A couple weeks later Lili called. She told me she is also a seamstress and is making a costume for herself and was planning to go to Venice at the end of February for Carnevale. And then she said that if I would like to go too she would make a costume for me and show me how to make a mask. Wow! Of course! The costume would be that of a *pierrot*, a French clown. I would wear heavy velvet trousers under a long satin cloak with an outsized bow at the neck, white gloves and of course the mask, and capped with a black beret. I gave her my measurements and she said it would all be ready for a fitting when I arrived.

I finally met Lili when I arrived on February 9, 1990 with all my stuff. Lili is from Santa Barbara and has been living in Aix a couple years. She's blonde, in her early 50s and fairly attractive. She is soft spoken, engaging, talented and smart. We proceeded with the fitting and she showed me how to make a papier mache mask. She left two days later and I moved in from my temporary hotel lodging. Within a week I found a fine apartment and moved again. After Lili returned Judy decided she would like to go to Venice as well. So the three of us, excitedly, prepared for this little adventure. And conveniently, I had the car, a leased 4-door Renault sedan.

Carnevale of course is on a Tuesday, the day before the beginning of Lent, as well as the several days leading up to it. So in high spirits we packed up the little Renault and drove off early into the Sunday morning sun. The scale of distance in Europe was so new to me. Even at a leisurely pace we drove half way across the South of France and all the way across the northern fat part of Italy in just eight hours.

Amazing! We parked the car in a garage in Maestre on the mainland and clambered with our luggage aboard a *vaporetto* (a boat that thinks it's a bus) that took us up the Grande Canale close to our hotel.

Lili had made the reservations and she had done very well. The small hotel was down a narrow street just two blocks from the front of San Marco, and in fact from our window we could look out and admire the splendid façade of this historic cathedral facing its grand Piazza. The room was large enough for three beds and somehow I was 'assigned' the middle one. In spite of the underlying temptations, we were all very considerate and most well behaved. Of course we were excited to be in Venice and quickly settled into our delightful new home.

Outside it was getting chilly as the moon was rising in the clear dusk of late February. And after a long and arduous day we were hungry and dry, so we eagerly went out to dinner. We spent two delightful hours at a fine restaurant enjoying local fish, pasta, dessert, and of course much vino. After we ambled home we sat and talked about tomorrow, what we would do and where we would go. And then it came time to prepare for bed, together with the swift evolving of social familiarity. On this night, each of us went into the bathroom to change into our proper nightwear. On the second night, after disrobing in privacy, we just came out and sat around in our underwear. On the third night all modesty disappeared. And as I recall, no one snored.

Lili and Len

It was Monday morning, clear and sunny, and after a leisurely breakfast in the hotel, we walked out into the maze of streets and canals to begin our exploration of this fabled city. Venice is a uniquely pedestrian city with many fascinating areas well off the beaten tourist track. And we were

determined to see and experience as many as we could.

It is easy to get lost in Venice, but what an opportunity to discover the unexpected. We spent the entire morning on the narrow streets and ancient bridges vaulting over myriad canals. We passed through quiet residential neighborhoods and mixed

with throngs of local shoppers at small open air markets. Finally, on the edge of exhaustion, we stopped for a fresh seafood lunch at a quaint little restaurant some-where, who knows exactly where, here in most hospitable Venice.

One of my traveling habits is to always carry a map, and so we were able to blunder our way back to the Piazza San Marco and to our hotel. We rested for an hour or so and then prepared to become part of the Carnevale. Lili donned her 'moon lady' costume and I became a believable *pierrot*, both of us with our papier mache masks. Judy chose not to costume and was content with a black 'Lone Ranger' mask.

And she offered to be the photographer, and would shoot off about 250 excellent photos. Now, properly dressed for the occasion, we ventured out, not as ourselves but as eager anonymous participants in an ancient tradition. We headed directly to the Piazza and found ourselves among hundreds of celebrants. Many wore extravagant costumes and elegant masks. And everybody walked slowly and quietly. It was bewildering. I had experienced the flamboyant gaiety and revelry of Mardi Gras in New Orleans, and was familiar with the raucous, samba-fueled Carnivales in Rio. But this was so very different. There was a pervasively quiet air of cautious serious-ness and secretive intrigue. Is this the evolved tradition spanning over four centuries from the time of Venice's prominence, noted for its conspiracies, murders, plots and betrayals in the quest for power? Puzzling. And to my astonishment, there was no music. None! Imagine!

The only sounds amid the footfalls on the pavement were the low murmurs of private conversations.

Yet I suppose, and would hope, the private parties and soirees behind these ancient walls are more boisterous and lively than anything here on the streets.

Once I had put on my mask I immediately noticed a change in my public behavior. I walked differently, slowly and deliberately, my head up and occasionally looking from side to side. I was completely anonymous and drawn to act the role I had assumed. I could pretty much, within reasonable limits of propriety, do whatever I pleased. Well, that was a heady new freedom that unexpectedly and happily added to these moments of enchantment.

On Tuesday, the final day before the beginning of Lent, the crowds of subdued revelers formed early, filling the piazzas, the streets and canals. Throngs of elaborately flamboyant costumes dazzled the eye, yet we in our modest outfits were still delighted to be able to participate in this ancient tradition. We wandered all over Venice, immersed in our understated charade. By mid afternoon we were exhausted and wearily retreated to our lodging for a welcome nap. But by early evening we were back on the streets. Restaurants everywhere were crammed full but we managed to slip in to a cozy neighborhood trattoria and enjoyed authentic down-to-earth Italian cuisine and hospitality. Finally, after even more street-walking and marveling at the eye-popping costumes around us, we were totally spent and headed back to our hotel. Earlier this morning the weather had dawned cool and misty, and under leaden skies the air was filled with an underlying threat of rain. But thankfully Venice had remained dry.

We slept till mid-morning when awakened by the clatter of city workers scurrying around clearing trash and cleaning up the deserted streets and piazzas. During breakfast we recapped all we had done during these hectic three days and emphatically agreed that this has been an extraordinary and uniquely memorable experience, as well as great fun. After check out, it began to rain as we hauled our luggage the three blocks to the edge of the Grande Canale for the *vaporetto* ride to Maestre and our car. And as we left the garage, the darkening skies burst and the rain became a torrential downpour, seeming like an appropriate coda to the pervasive gloom underlying this ancient festival known as the Carnevale di Venezia.

LEN VEITZER
November 2013

FINDING MY MUSE AND HOW I BECAME AN ARCHITECT

PART 1: BACKGROUND AND EARLY INFLUENCES

When I was really little I thought I would like to be a bird.

I vividly imagined flying, free as could be, and swooping and gliding and diving, and winging wherever I wanted to go. And then as a young boy I became entranced by airplanes. One time, on the inside of a large cardboard box, I carefully drew an instrument panel with dials and switches and would climb into the "cockpit" and spend hours pretending to be piloting a plane, together with my own sound effects. I could buy model kits for a dime and would spend countless hours building dozens of models with balsa wood and fast-drying glue and tissue paper and a long thick wound-up rubber band spinning the propeller, and the plane could fly! I excelled in high school mechanical drawing classes, had a good artistic eye and a skilled hand for freehand drawing. During those high school years I thought what I'd really like to do as a grown up is to design airplanes, that is, be an

Aeronautical Engineer.

Omaha Central High School

I had just turned 17 midway through my last year at Omaha Central High School when I signed up for the Naval Aviation Program known as V5. It would provide a four year college education, including Naval ROTC, at a major engineering school like Georgia Tech or Purdue. Upon graduation the candidate is enlisted in the Navy and sent to flight training school in Pensacola, and after commission as an Ensign and assigned flying duty, must remain in the Navy for at least three more years. This was just what I wanted. My application was accepted and I passed all the tests and physical exams. All that remained was an interview in Des Moines. And my parents' signature, as I was not yet 18. But my excitement and anticipation were summarily dashed when they refused to sign the papers. It was early in 1947, and the brutal war (WW2) had ended just a year and a half earlier. They just could not see their nice Jewish boy as an aviator, risking his life flying around in a Navy warplane, even in peacetime. Needless to say, I was angry and deeply disappointed. But I eventually got over it because shortly thereafter my folks announced that we will be moving to Los Angeles the day after my high school graduation. So I had a new focus --- exploring university possibilities in Los Angeles.

My parents, my 10 year old sister Nanie and I were on the train on June 1st, arriving in L.A. three days later. My folks had old friends from Chicago who owned some bungalows in Ocean Park, a small community between Santa Monica and Venice. We moved into one of them there on the corner of Surf Street and Speedway, a half block from the beach. This would be a temporary accommodation while my father looked for some kind of business. And here I was, this skinny, runty, very white kid suddenly perched on the edge of the vast Pacific, sensing for the first time the sounds and smells of the surf, and enviously watching the bronzed hunky guys plunging into the ocean, and very pretty girls looking very pretty. I knew I was on another planet, strange, exciting and yet so full of possibilities.

It took a few days for us to settle in and develop our own comfort levels and routines. I was anxious to start focusing on college possibilities, and USC and UCLA were the only schools I'd ever heard of in L.A. I quickly discovered that USC is a private school with high tuition so that was not a viable choice. On the other hand, UCLA being a state university, was highly respected and very affordable. I took the local bus to nearby Westwood and began to explore the campus.

It was a beautiful sunny day as I wandered about, admiring the impressive buildings and lovely landscaping. The walkways were filled with earnest summer school students as they hurried from class to class. It was all very impressive and so I found my way to the Administration Building and bought the catalog and class schedules. At the Admissions office I made inquiries, filled out paperwork, submitted my high school transcripts and arranged to take the admission exam. A few days later I took and passed the exam and a week after that I received notice of my acceptance as a freshman with instructions to enroll for classes in mid-September. Of course I was excited and overjoyed and the future looked good. Yes, very good.

About that time a brand new Sears Roebuck store had just been completed in Santa Monica at the west end of Olympic Blvd. and positions were available.

I applied and was hired to sell women's and children's shoes. I bought a beautiful new double-breasted suit, light gray with white chalk stripes. My salary was based on a 7% commission with a guaranteed minimum of $40/week [$417]**. I learned quickly, sold well, and was soon making $60-$70 [$626-730] weekly. My expenses were minimal so all my earnings were plunked into the bank. And all the while I'm excitedly anticipating UCLA in mid-September.

Toward the end of August my father was still looking for business opportunities and went to visit Joe Richlin, an old Chicago friend who years earlier had moved to San Diego. A few days later he returned to Ocean Park and announced that he had gone into a partnership with Joe to own and operate a trailer park in National City and that within a week we will be moving to San Diego. I was stunned! My plans for UCLA were dashed. Whoever heard of a college in San Diego? But my dad had learned that there is indeed a university there called San Diego State College. I was beside myself with anger. How could there be a "San Diego State College," I roared. Colleges weren't named after cities – they were named after states, like Ohio State, Oklahoma State, Michigan State and so on. In spite of my naïve complaints I soon came to realize I definitely had a lot to learn. Well, we moved in early September after I sadly withdrew from UCLA. We, the four of us, settled into a small house at 3688 Van Dyke St. in East San Diego (now called City Heights). I immediately went out to San Diego State to apply for admittance, was accepted and paid the $6.25 [$65] tuition fee. It was a small campus with 4,200 students, many of whom were returning veterans on the G.I. Bill. Most of the buildings were of the Mexican Revival style together with a few barracks and quonset huts left over from the war years, all spread out on the mesa. Football was played in Aztec Bowl, built into a hillside on the west edge of the campus in the '30s by the Government (WPA). And there was a calm and enveloping sense of ease and I quickly grew comfortable in this bucolic new environment under bright skies and temperate climate.

**[$00] indicates inflation-adjusted value to mid-2013.

I enjoyed my year at San Diego State, easily adjusting to California and college life. I made many new friends, including local Jewish students, and developed a minimal social life. The daily commute was a drag but I managed. I took up smoking a pipe because I thought it looked so cool. That all lasted about three months. The four of us were all comfortable enough in our modest little house on Van Dyke, which served our purposes well. What also still lingers so fondly in my memory is being out in our yard in the mild, mosquitoless, late autumn evenings and discovering the sweet aroma of night blooming jasmine.

Mechanical Engineering was the closest field of study to Aeronautical Engineering that the university offered so that became my major. My classes included physics, math, chemistry, surveying and P.E. My professors were good and I did well (As and Bs). That I was not in frigid Nebraska anymore was emphatically evident as I played touch football with my P.E. class under bright sunny skies in the middle of December in just shorts and a t-shirt. I could get used to this very easily and yes, I knew I would like it here.

It was a long haul to get to the campus from my house – an arduous six block walk to El Cajon Blvd. and then two buses. And the reverse on the return. But after a few weeks I arranged to ride with a classmate who also had an 8:00 o'clock class and who drove up El Cajon Blvd. He drove a '46 Ford coupe and would pick me up on the corner of El Cajon and Van Dyke, drive north on Fairmont and up Montezuma, a narrow 2-lane road to the campus. That helped alot.

During the Christmas break Joe Richlin's daughter came down from Berkeley where she was a student. We talked at length about campus life and she had very high praise for the College of Engineering at Berkeley. I had never heard of Berkeley let alone the University of California. But she was effusive in her praise of the campus at Berkeley and very persuasively suggested that I explore the possibility. I gave the idea some very serious thought and wrote for the catalog. It was such impressive reading that I began to make plans to visit Berkeley and see for myself. So it was mid-April during spring break when I boarded a Greyhound bus for the 14 hour trip to Berkeley. I checked into the Shattuck Hotel, bought a map and set out to explore the campus. I had never seen anything like it. It was breathtaking and it took me two exciting days to cover it all. And then I quickly knew that this is where I wanted to be.

I made inquiries at the College of Engineering, the University's Office of the Registrar, Admissions and the Housing office. I was there for most of the week and before returning to San Diego I made arrangements for the transfer of my high school and San Diego State transcripts and got the details of the required admissions exam, which I took and passed on a return trip during the summer. A week later I received my notice of admission as a sophomore to the University of California at Berkeley.

In early September I bade goodbye to my folks and Nanie and Greyhounded back to Berkeley. It was most economical to live and eat at one of the co-ops but there was no space available. But I could sign up for board (three meals a day) in exchange for three hours of work per week in the co-op. Then I rented a room in a small rooming house on Allston Way for $5/week [$52], about a mile from the co-op, the Engineering Building and the area where all my other classes would be. Tuition (fees) amounted to $35 [$365] per semester. Books about $30 [$315] and monthly expenses about $20 [$210]. My father was able to send me $70 [$730] a month. I was in General Engineering (again no Aeronautical specialty) and my classes included calculus, physics, chemistry, metallurgy and philosophy (an elective). They were all much more rigorous than anything I had experienced at San Diego State. I was quickly made to realize that I was in the big time now.

Because I lived so far away I was on or around the campus all day. I had to get up early, hike up to the co-op, have breakfast, pick up a bag lunch and get to my first class by 8:00. At the end of the day I'd be back at the co-op for supper and walk the mile back to my room by 7:00. I would settle in at my small desk and begin my homework but within an hour I was fading out. This was an impossible routine and as hard as I tried, I just couldn't keep up. I was exhausted and knew I was falling behind. And to make matters worse I had lost my enthusiasm. It was a lonely, unhappy, isolated existence. But then, during the third week, a really good thing happened.

I received an invitation in the mail to attend a rush party at the Sigma Alpha Mu (Sammy) fraternity house, one of the three Jewish fraternities on the campus. Joining a fraternity was not at all in my plans, in part because of the expense. But out of curiosity I went anyway. The house, a large white three-story building with public areas on the ground floor and many two-person and study rooms above was at 1735 LeRoy Ave. just two blocks north of the Engineering Building! In addition to the convenient location, I was particularly impressed by the gracious friendliness of the members there. And the other "rushees" were also open and sociable and seemed worth getting to know. A few were from out of state but most were from San Francisco and Los Angeles. I must have impressed as well because a few days later I received an invitation to join the fraternity and I could sense this rare and welcome opportunity. I decided to go for it.

But expenses were a serious limiting factor. In addition to a $50 [$520] "initiation fee," room and board was $75/mo. [$780] and I'd need $20 [$210] for incidental expenses. I wrote home, practically begging for $95/mo [$990], $25 more than my father was sending me. He was very reluctant but my mother, my lovely, loving, persuasive mama, prevailed, and full of excitement and anticipation I left the co-op and Allston Way and moved into the fraternity house.

Life was suddenly very different. I was one of 20 new "pledges," each of whom was assigned quarters in one of the several mini-dorms. Each man was also assigned a "big brother." And so I met Jerry Caris, an architecture major. There were three other arch majors who crammed their drafting tables into a cramped little room. In addition to Jerry there was Bernie Bloch, Stan Gould and Ray Kappe. And they would be working there every night until 1:00 or 2:00 o'clock, with classical music playing softly on the radio. When I'd finish my own engineering homework I'd pop in to visit with Jerry. What I discovered and admired was the kind of work they were all doing. What an eye opener! It was 1948 and they were designing in the "modern" idiom and their drawings were exquisite. I had never seen anything like it.

I slogged on with my studies but had a terrible time of it. It was harder than I ever imagined it would be. I soon came to realize that designing airplanes required more than drawing pictures and making models and mockups. The scientific rigors were far more than I anticipated or could handle. My first semester grades were an embarrassment – I had less than a C average and the University put me on probation, with the following semester to make up the deficiency.

I soon realized that I was not cut out to be an engineer. I needed to make a change. There was a guy in the fraternity named Arnold, a real jerk, from Atlanta whose father owned a large supermarket. Every week he would graphically lay out the full page ad with next week's sales, and mail it back to Atlanta. It took imagination, talent and a good eye and he was pretty good at all of it. I thought 'I could do that' and I began to give serious thought to a career in advertizing. But after spending several months among the 'architects' and their world it became clear that that was the path I could passionately embrace. I knew I had the innate talent and creative ability, and so, full of youthful optimism, I decided to pour myself into becoming an architect. It was the spring of 1949 and I had just turned 19. I withdrew from the College of Engineering and was accepted into the School of Architecture, where the curriculum dictated a four-year rigid sequence of classes, starting with Architecture 1, then Arch 2, 3, 4 and so on. Although I had completed two years of engineering, I could only get credit for the equivalent to Arch 2. I was enrolled in the Arch 1 class in September 1949, essentially starting over and looking at 3½ more years, and I was prepared to do that.

In the meantime I needed to raise my grades and complete this semester's courses. I was doing well until final exams, when I contracted mononucleosis. That knocked me out of three finals, which I took and passed three weeks later. My grades were not great but good enough to get me off suspension.

It was essential that I get a summer job because my father's support was drying up. He had left the trailer park business with Joe and bought a small variety store on Midway Drive. I was back in San Diego and could find nothing. I also tried architects' offices all over town but without any experience I was useless. September was approaching and I was forced to write to Berkeley and request a leave of absence. It was granted, for a year. Then, in early September, I did find a job! With an architect! His name was Richard Pinnell, a nifty guy in his mid-40s, with a tobacco stained mustache. He was running his practice on a shoestring but he was willing to take me on. His little office was at the end of an open corridor on a mezzanine inside an appliance store at 4th and Beech. One had to go through the store and up the stairs to reach his office. We were living on Hawley Blvd in Normal Heights and I would take the No. 11 bus down Adams and on to 4th and Beech. My limited drafting experience was all in engineering and I knew nothing about architectural drawing techniques, let alone how buildings are put together and what you call all those parts. Well, Pinnell was going to teach me and for the first week he offered to pay me $10 [$100}, and I was happy to take it. That first week I studied working drawings for small houses he had done, did some filing and got a sense of what an architect really did and how he did it. He must have been pleased with my progress because for the second week he paid me $15 [$150]. He had me start on a small 1-car garage as part of his current project and for the third week I made $20 [$200]. Over the next couple months I learned what goes into constructing a building and I became a fairly competent draftsman. My pay remained at $20/week (50 cents/hr [$5/hr]) until he just ran out of work for me and had to let me go just before Christmas.

I spent the next three weeks during the shopping season helping my father in the variety store. I stayed on for a couple more weeks taking inventory. Then in early March of 1950 I answered an ad to be a Federal Census Taker. One needed to be at least 21 years old but I was 20 and lied about my age. The pay would be 7 cents/head [70 cents]. During the first two weeks in April I canvassed half of Kensington. I conducted all interviews face to face and all data were entered by hand on provided forms. The supervisors were pleased with my efficiency and offered me the other half of Kensington, which I happily accepted and which lasted another two weeks. Since I was living at home and had no significant expenses, I was able to save a sizable chunk of money and looking forward to September back in Berkeley.

Three days after I finished with the census I spotted a help wanted ad in the paper for an "architectural draftsman." It was the office of a drafting service on the second floor of a building on First and Broadway downtown. I took the good old No. 11 bus the next morning together with a few rolls of drawings I had done for Pinnell. I entered into a small waiting room with a table, a couple chairs and a large filing cabinet. There were two other small rooms beyond, set up with drafting tables. The "draftsman" was a crusty old guy named Bohannon. He was not a licensed architect but "draftsmen" could prepare plans for houses without being licensed. And that's all he did – house plans. After he explained his system I showed him my work. He looked it all over carefully, pondered, and asked, "How much was the architect paying you?" I was too embarrassed to tell him 50 cents/hr [$5/hr] so I said sheepishly, "Not very much, because I was just starting out." He thought some more and said, "How about if I start you at $1.25 an hour?" [$12/hr]. I jumped at it and came to work the next day.

His work area was in one of the two small rooms and I worked in the other one. His operation was truly a drafting service. A client would come in, usually couples, and want to build a house on their just-purchased lot. Bohannon would inquire as to the details, like how many bedrooms, how many baths, what kind of roof they would like, preferred exterior materials and interior finishes, flat lot or sloping, raised floor or slab on grade, etc. Once he had all this information he would go to his filing cabinet and pull out bound files of single sheet floor plan and elevation blueprints meeting their requirements. He would lay these albums on the table and ask them to pore through them and pick out what they would like, and let him know when they had chosen something. Then he would excuse himself and retreat back into his office. The clients would leaf through their many possibilities and when they decided, they would call Bohannon back to the table and he would get the lot information and all their specific choices together with any other modifications and ask them to return in a week. Then he'd give all this to me to start drafting up a set of plans. When completed he would charge them $400 [$3,900] and give them four sets of blueprints. I worked for Bohannon until mid-September and made a bunch of money. I got a raise to $1.50/hr [$14/hr] and could turn out a <u>complete set of house plans in four days</u>.

I was 20 years old and still didn't have a car, nor did I even know how to drive. By summer we had moved to Guy Street, three blocks up the steep Andrews Street hill from the corner of Washington and India Streets. But now I was determined to learn to drive. My father's car, a '48 Plymouth, was always parked out in front. One Sunday morning at about 5 o'clock when everyone was still sound asleep, I snuck into my folks' bedroom and silently lifted the car keys from the dresser. I tiptoed out to the car and settled in behind the wheel. Over the last few years I had observed how my father drove and shifted gears and I tried doing it the same way. The Plymouth had a manual 3-speed transmission with the shifting lever on the steering column. I started the engine and slowly eased the car away from the curb and then down the steep Andrews Street. A sharp right turn and I was on Washington heading uphill to Mission Hills. Thankful that there was absolutely no other traffic that early on a Sunday morning, I carefully drove around Mission Hills for a few blocks, braking and clutching and sliding into the rhythm of shifting smoothly. After about 15 minutes I returned and silently parked in the same spot on Guy Street, carefully crept into the house, returned the keys to the dresser and went back to my room. Everyone was still asleep. A few days later I asked to borrow the car to go to the DMV for a driver's license. My dad said he didn't know that I knew how to drive but I assured him I did.

I contacted Berkeley for re-admittance and was re-scheduled for Architecture 1 in September of 1950. I moved back into the fraternity house and roomed with Bernie Bloch, who as newly elected president, had the primo second floor corner room. The Architecture Building was also on the north side and perfectly convenient. I did superbly well in Arch 1, getting the top grades. My other courses fared as well. At the end of the academic year I knew I was in my element. I loved what I was doing and accomplishing. Except for one B, I had all As. In the fall of 1951 I moved to the south side of the campus sharing a large room in an old craftsman house at 2610 College Avenue with Ron Russo, also an Arch major, and we became best of friends. We loved the imperial decoration of the two concrete lions flanking the entry steps. 60 years later, out of curiosity, I stopped by and sure enough they were still there.

I worked as a hasher (serving, bussing and set-up in exchange for meals) at the Alpha Phi sorority house, also on the south side. That year also went very well, with excellent grades and even better confidence in my abilities. Ron worked part time at a gas station and he knew cars. He found a '36 Dodge coupe for me which I bought for $35 [$300]. Again with his help I later traded up to a '41 Buick that had no grille but did have a radio. In the spring, Ron decided to live at home in San Francisco and I began looking for another place. I found a room, with a bathroom down the hall, in an old house on Tamalpais Road in a lovely quiet North Berkeley neighborhood. I arranged to hash at the Delta Phi Epsilon sorority house, next door to the Sammy house, and that arrangement worked out conveniently well.

And during Spring Break I worked for Bohannon in San Diego, accumulating needed money.

When the semester ended I returned to San Diego and got a summer job with Bob Bradt, an architect downtown in the Land Title Building on Second and Broadway. I did working drawings for several buildings, including a mausoleum in the Jewish section of the Greenwood Cemetery. Years later in 1980, after the funeral procession for my mother parked at Greenwood and I walked toward the mausoleum where the interment was to be held, I was suddenly struck dumb by how familiar that building looked to me. As I drew closer, I realized that I had done all the architectural drawings for this mausoleum! I reflected about this coincidence a long, long time. And still do.

I returned to the campus in September of 1952, eager to resume my studies. I moved back into the fraternity and settled in. And then, to my surprise and dismay, I received my draft notice to report for induction into the U.S. Army in San Diego on October 22. The war was still on in Korea and it looked like I was going to be part of it. The Buick was parked across the street with a dead battery and since I didn't know if I was ever coming back, I abandoned the car and gave the pink slip and keys to someone in the house. I packed up all my stuff, said my many goodbyes and boarded the Greyhound bus to San Diego, maybe for the last time. I was 22 years old.

It was during the Korean War when I was drafted into the U.S. Army on October 22, 1952 and Honorably Discharged on August 1, 1954. Most of my service was spent in Japan, which profoundly influenced my views and sensibilities on architecture, nature and the virtues of simplicity.

After then returning to San Diego I had a few weeks available before returning to Cal so I found a short term drafting job with Fred Liebhardt, a young and very talented architect. His office was in a funky old weathered wood cottage overlooking the Cove in La Jolla. He had spent a year at Frank Lloyd Wright's Taliesin West near Phoenix. His sensitivity to Japanese culture and design resonated so well with my own recent experiences that we became especially good friends, although I worked for him for just six weeks.

I also bought the blue '48 Plymouth from my father. When I returned to Berkeley in September to resume my architectural studies,

my Army service earned me the very helpful benefits of the G.I. Bill, which included tuition, fees, books and $110/mo. [$950/mo.] I was able to reconnect with Ron Russo. He had also been drafted and served in Germany and now he too was back in school. We were looking for a small apartment when I ran into Seymour Siegel, a fellow Pledge Class member from the fraternity. He was sharing a small apartment on Arch Street with two others. That's when I met Stu Greenfield and M.F. (Mack) McKamey, both returned from Korea and also Arch majors. We all decided to get together and rent a large house. Another Arch major, Rick Rice, joined us. We found a marvelous 3-bedroom house on Indian Rock Road in North Berkeley with a breathtaking panoramic view westward of San Francisco, the Bay and the magnificent Golden Gate Bridge, silhouetted against the fog beyond. Splitting the $150/mo. [$1,300/mo.] rent six ways was comfortably affordable. The six of us paired off, two to each bedroom. I roomed with Mack, who like me, was drawn to the simplicity and customs of Japanese culture. So we decided to replicate a tatami floor in our room. Tatami are woven straw floor mats, about one meter by two meters and about an inch thick with black fabric edging, and with a resilient infill. They are butted together and form the typical floor in Japanese homes. We bought 3x6 foot flat straw mats and enough carpet underpad for several layers. Mack sewed the straw mats together while I laid the underpadding, and when we laid the mats down on top it was just like a Japanese room. Instead of beds we just laid the mattresses on the floor. A couple small chests of drawers and we were back in Japan.

I was fortunate to be at Cal at this stage of the evolving modern movement. I benefited from mind-expanding teaching and on-the-mark critiques by superb professors. Most were older and favored the classicism of the French École des Beaux Arts tradition. Nonetheless, they knew, respected and emphasized the principles of good design, including scale, proportion, balance, composition and texture. They were experienced and mature and wisely able to apply these principles to their students' more contemporary designs. William Wurster, a highly respected and pioneering Bay Area architect was the Dean. The exceptionally fine faculty included Harold Stump, Kenneth Cardwell, Howard Moise, Warren Perry, Erich Mendelsohn, Stafford Jory and Vernon DeMars.

My major influences during this time of exploration and discovery were "The Big Three," Frank Lloyd Wright, Mies Van Der Rohe and Le Corbusier. The generally restrained, woody "Bay Area Style" also appealed to me, including the work of several leading local architects. Notably among them were Wurster, Bernard Maybeck, Joseph Esherick, Mario Ciampi, Jack Hillmer, Warren Callister and Worley Wong. I also admired the open planning and clean-lined, transparent work of several southern California architects like Richard Neutra, Gordon Drake, Rudolph Schindler, Harwell Hamilton Harris, Craig Ellwood, A.Q. Jones and Ed Killingsworth.

The School of Architecture ("The Ark") was located just inside the North Gate at Hearst and Euclid. The rambling one-story shingled building clambering up the slope parallel to Hearst Avenue was designed by John Galen Howard in 1906, and included administrative offices, design studios, a lecture hall, a large exhibition hall, a library and an extended gallery along the wide interior hallway. It was a hairy, creaky, charming environment.

I did extremely well in all my classes – three design projects each semester, architectural history, structural engineering, mechanical and electrical engineering, art and sculpture, and a couple electives. We all had a great time on Indian Rock Road but at the end of the semester we split up and decided to go our separate ways. It was now 1955 and I found a quaint little lower floor apartment in a house high up in the Berkeley Hills on Shasta Road that looked out to the west, providing an even broader view than that from Indian Rock Road. It was isolated, away from everything, but most of my days were spent on campus, and the semester went very well. I had excellent grades and my passion about architecture continued to grow. I longed to be able to design something real.

In the fall I moved back into town and took an apartment on the ground floor of an old Victorian on Dwight Avenue next to the Herrick Hospital. This was to be my last semester and I had only the last design class left to do. I did exceptionally well and in fact as the projects were being critiqued and graded in open session by the faculty, my design was most highly praised and received the top grade among my 16 other classmates. I returned home later that evening, ecstatic. The events of the evening confirmed what I already believed – that I had a genuine design talent and would be a fine and creative architect. I was so proud and full of myself when I went to bed, and so energized, that I couldn't fall asleep.

And that is when I had what could best be described as an epiphany.

As I lay there imagining what a fine creative architect I would be, it suddenly occurred to me that I had within me another, more profound creative power. I could help to make people. After all, how could even the most magnificently beautiful building begin to compare with a human life? A real person? And so I resolved, then and there in the midst of my self-absorption, that when I married and my wife was of a like mind, we would have as many children as we could. And with that settled I fell blissfully asleep.

I had been working concurrently as a part time draftsman for Joe Smoot, a young home designer in Orinda, through the tunnel just east of Berkeley. Joe was a good sensitive designer. I enjoyed working there in his rustic quarters and was glad to help him even as I was honing my own skills. I was a good draftsman and it brought me some welcome income.

At the same time I connected with the Frandsens who wanted to build a house in Danville.

Mr. and Mrs. Martin Frandsen
Danville CA

It was late in 1955 and I was in my last semester in the School of Architecture at Cal in Berkeley. It was a policy of the School to assist students by posting on a bulletin board requests from private parties who wanted some cheap architectural design. It was a popular program and the notices were quickly gobbled up. One afternoon I was looking at the very few postings when the secretary came out and tacked up a new one. I glomped onto it immediately.

This retired couple had some land in Danville (farther east of Berkeley) and wanted to build a small house. I arranged to meet them at their property and drove out the 25 miles in my '48 Plymouth. Danville was not yet developed and was still mostly rural. This magnificent site was a level seven acre grove of walnut trees 30 feet apart in both directions. I drove in toward a little clearing where one of the trees had been removed and where this elderly couple were waiting.

And here is where I met the Frandsens. We sat and talked for a long time as we gradually became comfortable with each other. I took many notes about what they wanted in a house, area limits, and their lifestyle. What was most important and surprising to me was that he wanted to build it himself! We quickly came to like each other and, importantly, I had their full confidence. We agreed on a fee of $400 [$3,400] for design and full working drawings. I took a few photos and drove back to Berkeley with an excitement never before experienced. This will be my first <u>real</u> house!

I completed a preliminary design and drawings in a couple weeks and met them at their home. They loved what I had done and were as excited as I was. I returned to my drafting table in my Berkeley apartment anxious to begin the working drawings. I still had school projects and other homework to attend to, but in about a month I refined the design, worked out all the details and completed the working drawings. This was going to be a lovely house.

When I proudly and happily presented the drawings and explained all the details, I watched with growing alarm the change in Mr. Frandsen's demeanor. He fell silent and I knew something was the matter. He finally acknowledged, that although he understood the design and the details, it was just too complicated for him to build. I was shocked and felt remorseful that I had let him down. I paused for a minute or two and told him I'll retain the same concept but simplify the design, prepare new drawings and be back in a week.

I modified and simplified the design, actually an improvement, and prepared an entire new set of working drawings in five days! When he saw the new plans, his warm smile returned with his optimism, for now he could build this fine home for him and his dear wife. I visited the site three or four times during construction but left Berkeley when the framing was almost completed. The house was looking really good!

I was in Berkeley a couple years later and drove out, full of anticipation, to visit the Frandsens. The house had become a home and was simply beautiful, diminutively nestled there in the midst of all those walnut trees. He had built it with skill and passion. And the two of them were so happily settled in. There is no way I can describe the joy I felt for this lovely and contented couple, as well as the satisfaction for my contribution.

I lost touch with the Frandsens after that last visit and don't know whether they sold the property or had passed on. Because years later, burgeoning development altered the bucolic setting of Danville, including a particular grove of walnut trees and the simple, lovely house among them.

By January of 1956, after a rocky start and a very long haul, I had completed all my academic work and graduated from the University of California, Berkeley with a B.A. in Architecture, summa cum laude.

THE REGENTS OF THE UNIVERSITY OF CALIFORNIA

ON THE NOMINATION OF THE FACULTY OF
THE COLLEGE OF ARCHITECTURE
HAVE CONFERRED UPON

LEONARD MENDEL VEITZER

THE DEGREE OF BACHELOR OF ARTS
WITH ALL THE RIGHTS AND PRIVILEGES THERETO PERTAINING

GIVEN AT BERKELEY THIS TWENTY-SIXTH DAY OF JANUARY
IN THE YEAR NINETEEN HUNDRED AND FIFTY-SIX

GOVERNOR OF CALIFORNIA AND
PRESIDENT OF THE REGENTS

PRESIDENT OF THE UNIVERSITY

CHANCELLOR AT BERKELEY

DEAN OF THE COLLEGE

LEN VEITZER
October 2013

FINDING MY MUSE AND HOW I
BECAME AN ARCHITECT

PART 2: DISCOVERING THE PASSION

I was 26 years old, free, restless, and desperately wanted to travel. I had written to many agencies about architectural employment abroad, but to no avail. So I made plans to do it on my own. I was an excellent draftsman, and with construction booming, I could easily get a job anywhere. I wanted to drive first to New Orleans in time for Mardi Gras, and work a few months. Then out to Sarasota, Florida where a few very good young architects were producing a growing number of fine contemporary schools and houses. Then I would motor up to New York, work for a year or so, and head on to Europe for more adventure and whatever work I could find. In order to begin accumulating some money after my graduation I got a job in Berkeley in February of 1956 with a fine architect, Morgan Shaw, whose specialty was shopping centers. He had been a navigator on a B17 in the air war over Germany and had harrowing stories to tell. I was among three draftsmen in the office and I produced very well. In late October when I told Morgan I was leaving to return to San Diego, he offered me an associateship (whatever that meant). I was very flattered but too anxious to begin my odyssey.

On November 1st I packed up the old Plymouth and returned to my parents' home at 4460 48th St. in San Diego. I quickly got a job downtown with 'Pat' Paderewski, Mitchell and Dean, one of the major firms in town. I told them I could stay for only three months but they were glad to have me and give me a position. They were doing larger buildings of all kinds but a friend of Paderewski's wanted a new house and Pat couldn't turn him down. So he gave it to me. I was there for the three months and completed the design and working drawings for the project. I had done a good job and it turned out well. Pat was happy and so was the client. I made some good friends while there and was able to bank a few bucks for my upcoming journey.

I was now ready to begin taking the rigorous Architectural State Board exams, which are given twice a year, to become a licensed architect in the State of California. In order to be eligible to take all seven sections of the exams, a candidate must have a minimum of seven combined years of an architectural degree and practical working experience with a licensed architect. However, with a degree and at least one year of practical experience one could take the first half of the exams. And I qualified for that and planned to go to Los Angeles for a couple days in mid-December and take the first four sections (site planning, architectural history and theory, mechanics of materials and structural design). Subsequently after one passes all seven parts of the exam, an oral exam would be the final step. A daunting process indeed. But I had never a doubt that I could do it.

In addition to working and studying for the exams, I was building a hi-fi system (long before stereo) from scratch. I learned electronics in the army and found very good schematics for an amplifier and a preamplifier in an electronics magazine. I bought all the parts (capacitors, resistors, tubes, wiring, etc.) and a soldering iron and began to assemble. I also built a 38" high plywood speaker box for an 8" speaker. But I did have to buy a turntable and cartridge to complete the system. I also had been accumulating 12" long play vinyl records of favorite and new classical and jazz music. The system turned out well and worked perfectly, which was good because I wanted to take it all with me on my travels.

In the meantime, I met Nadene Feiler.

It was shortly after I arrived home from Berkeley when our mothers, as mothers sometimes do, schemed to have us meet. We immediately liked each other and started dating, and by the end of the year our relationship had gotten very serious. But I remained blindly undeterred from my planned travels. Economic times were good and with my extensive drafting experience I knew I could get a job anywhere. So on a bright early morning in mid-January my trusty Plymouth was fully packed and gassed, and after many hugs and kisses and tearful goodbyes, I was off to see the rest of the world.

I was in New Orleans four days later and temporarily settled in at the Sammy house at the Tulane University campus. I soon moved into a nice little ground floor apartment (at the sidewalk) of an 1832 building at 532 Gov. Nicholls St. in the French Quarter. The rent was $55/mo. [$455]. The next day, four days after my 27th birthday,

I found a job with Ricciuti Associates, an architectural firm on Royal Street. It was a good place to work and I loved New Orleans. Nadene and I wrote longingly back and forth and by the beginning of April I knew I was deeply in love with her, missed her terribly and didn't want to be without her. I gave notice to Ricciuti, flew back to San Diego on April 13 and proposed. She happily accepted, and we were married by rabbi Baruch Stern in a small family ceremony on April 24, 1957.

A week later with the Plymouth all packed we were on our way to Sarasota, which was a small city on the Florida Gulf Coast. We rented a small Alpine style house for $55/mo. [$455] on a half-acre near the Ringling Bros. Circus headquarters. It seemed so out-of-place there in the tropics, a log cabin with a great stone fireplace and an interior loft under a high pitched roof. Once we managed to cope with the mosquitoes we were happy there. I was hoping to work for Paul Rudolph, a brilliant young architect designing some stunning houses and schools. He had a tiny office and slept in the back room, but was in a dry spell and had no positions open. In the next few years he would become a star with major published buildings and eventually become Dean of the College of Architecture at Yale University. So instead I found a job in a small office with architect Harvey Jernigan, who had a modest practice with relatively small projects.

Nadene and I liked Sarasota in spite of the discomforting summertime heat and humidity and the voracious mosquitoes. We also acquired our (my) first dog, a puppy we called Woofie, equal parts Boxer and Collie.

We stayed until September, and after a couple weeks in Havana visiting relatives, we motored to New York. We settled into a fourth-floor furnished one bedroom walkup apartment at 239 East 60th Street between 2nd and 3rd Avenues, just off the Queensborough Bridge. The rent was a staggering $150/mo. [$1,240].

I applied for a position at Harrison and Abramovitz, an old and widely respected architectural firm responsible for many high rises in Manhattan, classrooms and chapels at Brandeis University and many other noteworthy buildings in the Northeast. Their staff of about 150 occupied an entire floor of the International Building in Rockefeller Center, across the street from St. Patrick's Cathedral. I went home and two days later, on September 30, received a telegram inviting me to join the firm with a generous salary of $140/week [$1,200]. Nadene was a superb typist and got a job at Booz Allen Hamilton (business efficiency consultants), not far from Rockefeller Center. We both walked to work and frequently had lunch together. Harrison was on the Board of the Museum of Modern Art so everybody in the office had a pass. Nadene and I visited and lunched there often.

Living in New York City was an exciting and stimulating experience for us. After a month of getting parking tickets I took the Plymouth to a parking garage in Queens, a 15 minute bus ride from our home. We walked everywhere and explored as much as we could. A long walk from our mid-town apartment all the way down to Greenwich Village and back on a beautiful Saturday morning was more than memorable. We were able to watch the ongoing construction of Wright's Guggenheim Museum and Mies van der Rohe's Seagram Building. And many weekend afternoons were spent at the Metropolitan Museum.

On the Thanksgiving weekend we drove up with Woofie to visit Boston but could not find a motel in Boston and ended up in Salem. It was so cold while sightseeing that even though we were bundled up we kept having to retreat to the car to thaw out. But winter in New York was magnificent and easy to get used to. We spent New Year's Eve with friends in a restaurant in Chinatown, throwing ourselves at the mercy of the waiter to feed and delight us.

The office had begun master planning The Lincoln Center for the Performing Arts and awarding design commissions for the various buildings that would comprise this very important cultural complex. The principal building would be The Metropolitan Opera House, and Wally Harrison would be the architect. Max Abramovitz would design Philharmonic Hall for the New York Philharmonic Orchestra. Notable architects would design the several other buildings. For the first few months in the office I was among many others drafting working drawings for major projects in Manhattan, including The New York Daily News Building. I must have done well and shown some talent for

I was tapped to assist Harrison on the design of the Opera House. I worked for weeks on the front façade providing rendered elevations, sections and perspectives from Harrison's rough sketches. So many different schemes, and after many trials and rejections, finally the five-arch choice, finely tuned, tweaked and massaged to have the most pleasing scale and proportions. And that façade is what ultimately was built, the iconic image of Lincoln Center.

This firm was such a wonderful place to work and I learned so much. My few years' of prior experience had been primarily with houses and other small scale projects. This provided me the opportunity to observe and experience the organization and professional ability that went into the design and production of construction drawings for very large buildings. I felt very fortunate, and still do, that I had the rare opportunity to be there.

In the meantime, issues with the California Board of Architectural Examiners began to loom. Their rule was that a candidate could take the exams, which were scheduled every six months, as often as needed to pass all the parts. However, if one missed three testing times in a row, all parts previously passed would be forfeited. My travels had bypassed two testing dates and the critical third test was to be in early July. I had passed three of the hardest exams and had to retake the Site Planning portion, which I had failed earlier. Although I was not yet eligible for the other three remaining parts, I was not going to forfeit everything I'd passed and have to start all over again. Flying back and forth in those days was just too darned expensive. So in late spring we began to make plans to return to California.

So in mid-May we bade farewell to New York and friends we had made, packed up our faithful Plymouth, and Nadene, Woofie and I headed out. There was no immediate urgency and so we decided to take our time. We drove up to Niagara Falls and then across to visit relatives in Toronto. We stayed a couple days and then motored westward in Canada to Windsor and Detroit. We got to Omaha in early June and stayed about a week, revisiting relatives, old friends and familiar places. It was a warm sunny Saturday afternoon when we checked into a motel in Colorado Springs. After we had visited the Air Force Academy, which was under construction, we were sitting around the pool at the motel when Nadene became dizzy, and after I carried her up to our room, she told me that we are going to have a baby! We were both thrilled! By evening she was okay and by the time we left in the morning we had decided to abandon our leisurely meandering pace and head directly to San Diego. This had been such an interesting and enjoyable drive from New York and even Woofie traveled very well. We arrived at her parents' house at 6076 Crawford Street, unloaded our car, and my folks and Nanie hurried over to greet us. We talked for hours, entertaining the Feilers and Veitzers with our tales of discovery and adventure. And then when we casually mentioned our good news, great elation and glee burst forth. It was an especially joyous and happy homecoming.

In late June I drove up to L.A. and took the Site Planning exam and was notified two months later that I had passed.

We settled in for a temporary stay; even Woofie was happy to be able to run around the big yard. But there were three immediate tasks to address. First we met with Joe Kwint, a warm and sensitive, highly recommended obstetrician/gynecologist. Nadene was healthy and in good condition and we could expect our first child in January. But we also needed a place to live and I needed to find a job. We decided to try to buy a house and began looking in Kensington, an area I admired from my census-taking days. That was our first choice but out of our price capability. But we needed something. There were the dreaded tract developments being built all over the city and through the G.I.

Bill I could get a low interest loan. I was being gradually worn down and although I abhorred the idea, we began looking at tract houses. And the longer we looked the more discouraging it all became, and an ominous sense of desperation surfaced. We finally found a group of houses under construction in a neighborhood just east of Sharp Hospital called Serra Mesa. They had plain exteriors and simple decent floor plans, and because they were in the framing stage I could observe that they were being built well. And time was running short so, with many misgivings and as a last resort, we bought one at 2674 Russmar Drive with three bedrooms, two baths, hardwood floors and plaster walls and ceilings, and no landscaping. We moved in around Thanksgiving.

And then ……….

The first time thrill of eagerly anticipated fatherhood enveloped me with a deep emotional fulfillment upon the birth of Ian Matthew, our first child, on January 13, 1959.

In the meantime I had made many inquiries and found a good job with Dale Naegle, a fine architect who had a small office on Avenida de la Playa in La Jolla Shores. It was a long and difficult commute, either through Clairemont on a rocky unpaved Balboa Avenue or by way of the eight mile stretch of two-lane Miramar Road. Over the next 18 months my brave old Plymouth took a terrible beating. Dale was a very good designer and working for him was a real pleasure. I drafted working drawings on many small projects and had a chance to design a couple small houses as well. Dale was a tall gangly guy about five years out of USC. He had been crippled by polio as a youngster but he didn't let that slow him down, particularly in his '56 T-bird convertible.

In the Fall of 1959 Roy Wieghorst, an old army buddy, called and asked if I would design a new house for him and his wife Barbara on a hillside in El Cajon.

I met Roy when we were both drafted into the army at the same time in 1952. In basic training at Ft. Bliss, Texas we formed a strong friendship, which we maintained in San Diego after being discharged in 1954. He married Barbara a few years later and Nadene and I would visit with them from time to time.

What an exciting prospect that was to be! I met them at his parent's home in the southern hills of El Cajon. Roy's lot was just next door, a sloping acre with glorious views over the city and the foothills and mountains beyond. There were no other developments around anywhere and they could ride their horses all over the neighborhood. It was quiet, isolated and bucolic. The site was without trees and was covered with low brush and several clusters of gray granite rock.

Roy's father, Olaf, had been a cowboy in his early years, and had become an internationally recognized painter of western life --- cowboys, horses, Indians. Roy grew up in this environment and had developed a strong preference for a rustic, rough-hewn character for his house. This was going to be my first house in San Diego and I was full of creative energy, but concerned about changes during construction to my carefully thought out details. So when it was time to establish my fee, I proposed the following: no cost at all, with the proviso that the house be built exactly as drawn and detailed, and without deviation. Roy found that an offer he couldn't refuse. I set up my old college drafting table in the spare bedroom and worked on their house during evenings and weekends.

Roy and Barbara wanted a small house, as they had no children. Two bedrooms, one bath, kitchen, dining and living rooms and no garage. These would fit their budget and immediate needs. After a couple visits to the site, a concept began to evolve: A long narrow house with two parallel retaining walls parallel to the slope, and a flat area in between for the structure.

The retaining walls were of reinforced concrete block sheathed inside and out with granite rock quarried from the site. Structural elements included concrete slab on grade, wood wall framing, exposed wood beams and exposed incense cedar roof decking.

Exterior and interior wall finishes were rough-sawn western red cedar vertical siding and the roof was of heavy wood shake shingles. The north and east walls accessing the views were entirely of glass, either fixed or in French doors. The house is low-slung and embedded into the hillside. It is essentially wood, stone and glass. Its character is rough, solid and compatible with its natural setting.

Because I had learned it all very well in school and was sure of my competence, I did all the structural calculations as well as those for heating, air conditioning and electrical. Joe Yamada was the landscape architect and Diane Powers of the Design Center designed and furnished the interiors.

Roy had a friend, an older man named Carl Kaland, who truly was a skilled master carpenter. Except for specialized trades like plumbing, heating, stone masonry, electrical and roofing, he and Roy together built the house. Kaland was one of those rare old school craftsmen; all the wood framing was not only nailed, but glued. The wood siding was all blind-nailed (you can't see the nails) and the mitred corners looked like a solid piece of wood. And after decades of use, everything is still straight, plumb and without any sign of age. A rare testament to skill and quality.

Years later, with the arrival of Dana and Lisa to the family, I designed, for a fee, an addition expanding the house northward with a new dining room, powder room and master bedroom and bath, all integrated seamlessly with the original house. Over the years the children grew up and moved on. Roy and Barbara still live there in retired comfort. They love their house, as it has served them so perfectly well all these years. And to my proud satisfaction, the original house and addition were built exactly as designed.

Toward the end of 1959 a realtor friend of mine, Marvin Zigman, and Bob Casey, a tract home developer, asked me if I'd be interested in designing the first office building in Mission Valley. I was still working for Dale Naegle and had just completed the plans for the Wieghorst House while 'moonlighting' at home. I was not yet licensed but it seemed like a rare and wonderful opportunity – one I just couldn't pass up. It was exciting and I was supremely confident. I was about to take the final section of the State Board exams in December but wouldn't learn the results until February. Then, if I passed, I would take the orals a month later. That's what ultimately happened, and after passing the orals I became licensed in California (No. C-3043) in April of 1960. Until then, I could not represent myself as "architect." But it was not uncommon then for a "draftsman" to prepare drawings for a building larger than a house by hiring a structural engineer to do the structural design and who would then sign the plans. And that is what I intended to do.

And now finally, after years of dreaming and anticipation, I was about to have my own architectural office.

Bernard Lewis prepared a contract for me for full architectural services. I was identified as "Draftsman" and my fee was to be 4% of the cost of construction. [The AIA Standard Fee for that type of building was 7-8%]. With a signed contract in hand and a $500 [$4,000] retainer, I set out to rent an office. I found the perfect spot on the northwest corner of Fifth Avenue and Upas Street in Hillcrest.

I leased half of the upper floor of a two-story converted residence at 440 Upas Street (until recently the site of the Blood Bank). I set up a work space with two drafting tables and a reception/secretary area. It was bright and airy and I would be there for three years.

The three acre sloping site was on the south side of Interstate 8 just west of Ward Road in Mission Valley. There were no other buildings around there. No shopping centers. No auto dealers. The only hotel was the Town and Country Hotel about a mile west. The building program called for a three-story wood frame structure of approximately 25,000 square feet. I prepared an elegant design with two parallel wings flanking an open landscaped atrium in between. Aluminum sunscreens shielded the east and west walls. Parking was on grade in the front and rear of the building. The design was enthusiastically received by Zigman and Casey, and I was authorized to begin the construction documents. I engaged Tom Atkinson for structural engineering and Joe Roberts for mechanical and electrical engineering. I also hired architect Dan Perkins to prepare spec-ifications. Ken Kellogg did much of the drafting. I designed all the details, coordinated all the consultants and checked all the drawings.

Shortly after completion of all the drawings and specifications, Zigman and Casey began to have financing concerns and decided to suspend the project pending outcome of a rezoning study of Mission Valley by the City Planning Department. Although I had completed all the drawings and specifications, they continued to stall payment of the $13,000 [$102,000] balance of my fee. I was compelled to file a lawsuit demanding payment, and Mickey Fredman, their lawyer, met me with my attorney Bernard Lewis on the courthouse steps on the way to trial and handed me a certified check in the full amount. Of course I was happy to be paid but deeply disappointed after pouring so much design energy into this building. But there were lessons to be learned about expectations and uncertainty, and projects "that never get built."

Although the City Planning Department's zoning review turned out to be favorable, Zigman and Casey decided to sell the property to Ben Kolkey and Dass Construction Company, who were tract home developers. Dass then hired me to redesign the project and renamed it "Mission Square."

I was soon notified by the State Board that I had now passed all the required exams and was scheduled for the orals in Los Angeles on April 3, 1960. I passed that as well. And then, after a long, long slog ....

I finally became an Architect licensed in the State of California (C-3043)

I then joined and became an active member of the American Institute of Architects (AIA) and printed up stationery and business cards.

LEN VEITZER
November 2013

LA CORRIDA

In 1990 I was living in the South of France in Aix-en-Provence and made the acquaintance of a lovely and genial French woman named Catherine. One spring day she asked me if I would like to attend the bullfights in Arles on Easter Monday, when the French joyously celebrate their three-day Easter weekend. Six corridas are scheduled each day of Easter Weekend: Novices on Saturday, Intermediates on Sunday and the Top Professionals on Monday. The matadors are all Spanish and the bulls are bred and raised on Spanish rancheros. After the Easter Weekend, corridas are held every Sunday afternoon throughout the summer until September.

I had lived in San Diego most of my life but never watched a bullfight in nearby Tijuana, a vibrant city of over 700,000 just across the border. On Sunday afternoons during the season either of the city's two bullrings would be packed with passionate aficionados. But I never went, not for reasons of conscience but more out of a sense of indifference. So with this unexpected opportunity I eagerly accepted Catherine's invitation, and a week later we drove westward in the sunlit morning after Easter, past verdant farms and through quiet villages, and arrived mid-morning just as Arles, after two days and nights of revelry, was beginning to awaken.

The ancient city of Arles, straddling the River Rhone, is but an hour's drive from Aix. It is also noted as the home of Vincent Van Gogh for two years where he produced much of his most memorable and admired work. Arles' population of 52,000 swells during the summer months beginning with Easter Weekend because that's when the bullfight season begins. The Spanish border is but 160 miles to the south and the influence of Spain over the centuries has had a lasting effect on the life and culture of Arles. From Easter until the first weekend of September the city transforms. Fiestas abound. The shops and bodegas feature colorful Spanish merchandise and elegant wear. Spanish music fills the air. Throngs of festive diners fill the restaurants to enjoy genuine Spanish cuisine. And this all begins on Easter Weekend, ushered in each year by the bullfights in the revered 2,000 year old Roman Coliseum, right there in the center of the city.

After we parked our car we found our way to the ticket window in the side of the Coliseum. I had been a little concerned because Monday's corridas would be the most popular and Catherine had not pre-purchased tickets. But  she assured me it would not be a problem. And of course she was right. We purchased our tickets straight away and since the first corrida would not be until 4:00 o'clock, we strolled about, poking into the many bodegas and specialty shops. About mid-day our appetites directed us to the iconic Place du Forum, a large square a few blocks from the Coliseum, where we could have lunch. It too was transformed. The magnificent 30 foot plane trees bordering the square cast dappled sunlight through their new spring growth. The normally open area was today filled with large tables and chairs and festive folks milling about savoring the enticing aroma of the spicy,

 saffron-laced paella being prepared in the traditional flat one meter round pans by chefs from the three restaurants on the square. Soon the queues formed and for nominal cost generous portions of paella on paper plates and pitchers of sangria appeared on the tables. From somewhere in the square guitars and trumpets played lively Spanish music. The gaiety of so many joyous people on this warm spring day was seductive and infectious, and Catherine and I immediately immersed ourselves in its midst. It was two o'clock by the time we had gorged and besotted ourselves on the delicious paella and the hearty sangria. As we left, the fiesta was continuing in full force with happy new celebrants. We spent some more time wandering about the city, exploring the side streets and nearby Roman ruins.

Around 3:30 we entered into a long dark tunnel that carried us through the bowels of this ancient Coliseum, bursting suddenly into the blindingly sunlit arena. Circling the arena were rows upon rows of massive granite blocks, the seating for 20,000, rising up to the ramparts. We found our seats and settled in to await the pageantry. My mind began to wander backward and wonder who were the people who sat on this very same cold hard seat during countless events over the last twenty centuries. And what were they watching? [A few months later I was once again in this Coliseum in Arles attending a sold out Ray Charles concert]

By 4:00 o'clock the Coliseum was packed, and while the trumpets blared, the brightly costumed participants marched out and paraded to thunderous shouts and applause. Soon after, the sandy field was empty and all became quiet and the air was electric in anticipation of the first corrida. The trumpets sounded again and suddenly a gate opened. Out charged this huge magnificent bull, its head held high with noble grace. He seemed confused as he looked around to get his bearings but then began to run about. The crowd cheered. Then the picadores rode out on their armored horses and began their grisly work. Soon, amid thunderous applause, the torero appeared. His skill and bravery were displayed with his elegant capework against the charging bull. And the multitudes roared with oles with each graceful pass.

Then suddenly, during a daring maneuver, the torero was hooked and thrown violently over the bull's head. The crowd gasped and went eerily silent as the bull was distracted enough to allow rescuers to help the seriously wounded bullfighter off the sand and to the infirmary. The angry bull continued to roam the arena, chasing young novices trying to display their courage. After about ten minutes and accompanied by thunderous acclaim, the bandaged torero returned to the arena. It was time for the kill. This once magnificent beast, its head now down, bleeding and slobbering, stood dazed and motionless. The bullfighter aimed and plunged his sword deep, but missed the fatal spot. The bull stood, unfazed. Twice more the torero thrust. And twice more this noble animal would not go down. Then the tenor of the crowd changed, demanding that the bull be spared. The judges agreed and amid tumultuous approval the triumphant bull was led, bloody and battered, from the arena. So now the bulls were leading one to nothing.

In the ensuing corridas, amid all the trumpetry and pageantry, the remaining five brave bulls were efficiently dispatched by five brave men, as expected. But what was most memorable to these 20,000 people was that stalwart first bull they had demanded be spared. But even that, alas, was short lived. As Catherine and I left and walked around the coliseum, we passed a brightly lit area beneath the great structure with a half dozen refrigerated trucks waiting outside. Inside the illuminated area were six hanging carcasses being butchered by white-coated men. It was immediately clear that six bulls were contracted for and six bulls were being delivered.

On the drive back to Aix, we talked about the entire day, from exploring this beautiful and ancient city to the superb lunch in the Place du Forum, and then of course the bullfights. When she asked me what I thought of them, I was given pause to reflect. And I told her that even though they are not mine, I can respect the values of certain traditions to a culture. My impressions were decidedly mixed but for disparate reasons. I had come away with both sheer admiration and abject repulsion. In Spain the celebrated tradition of corrida has evolved into a perilous art form of ballet-like grace, beauty and consummate skill. It has never bothered me that all over the world animals are killed for consumption. But killing for sport, like what I witnessed that day, I have always found abhorrent. Yet it was not the death of these bulls that disturbed me so much as, in just over just a few minutes, the cruel degradation that transformed these strikingly beautiful and powerful creatures into pathetic, blithering and pitiful remnants of their former selves. So very sad. Beyond dreadfully sad.

And yet there is the willingness, in fact eagerness, of some men to face death in order to validate their mastery of life. Because people love to observe dangerous feats of bravery and courage, these men choose to display their fearlessness by testing how close they can come to escaping a painful death or serious injury by performing brilliantly with exquisite grace, and then finally basking in the glory of triumph and the adulation of thousands.

And I can admire and appreciate all that.

But not the appalling, ugly, repugnant desecration of the noble and gallant Toro. Both forces are present and integral as if contending for dominance – the sublime and the profane, both part of the ritual of La Corrida.

LEN VEITZER
November 2013

KOS

In late 1975 my wife Nadene and I were ready to take our first trip to Europe. We were planning to spend four weeks exploring the Greek mainland as well as many of the Aegean Islands as possible. Because we would be on our own, we prepared extensively, studied maps and tour books, reviewed my architectural history, and learned the alphabet and the essential words of courtesy. We would be travelling during the winter to avoid the tourist season, and we'd take our chances with the weather.

We lived near San Diego State University and just a few days before departure I stopped for a quick lunch at a Greek café adjacent to the campus. I got to talking with the young Greek waiter serving me. With growing interest he asked what islands I was planning to visit, and his eyes lit up when I mentioned Kalymnos and Kos because he was from the island of Kos. He had had a bitter and terrible falling out with his father and abruptly left home and made his way to America. He had not written since then and ended up here at San Diego State where he was about to graduate. But he became very excited as we talked about my visit to Kos. He wistfully asked if I would take a letter with me for his family and I said I would be happy to, but hurry, because we are about to leave. The next day I went back to the café and picked up his letter together with the address on the front. His deep, sad eyes betrayed his melancholy.

Weeks later, early on a crisp and sunny morning in mid-January, Nadene and I boarded a ferry in Rhodes and headed north for the five hour journey to the small island of Kos. It is in the Dodecanese chain of islands in the eastern Aegean Sea, four kilometers off the western coast of Turkey. Kos is a long island, 40 km by 8 km, and with a population of about 30,000. It had been an important commercial center during the prominence of classical Greece in the time of Pericles 25 centuries ago, and was particularly noteworthy as the home of Hippocrates, considered one of the most outstanding and influential figures in the history of medicine. It has had a turbulent history since then and now, except for the port city of Kos Town, it is rural with small farms and a few isolated villages. Kos Town is popular with tourists, but beyond the town, life on this island is very difficult and primitive. The people are very religious and are still steeped in their entrenched, traditional ways. "Progress" here seems to advance at an extremely slow crawl.

We disembarked, and after lunch at a taverna along the quai, we hired a taxi to take us to the family of the young Greek student in San Diego. The driver knew no English but when I showed him the letter with the address, he knew exactly where to go. We drove for an hour up into the hills through hard-scrabble farmlands and scraggly forests. When we finally arrived at this small village with dirt streets and telephone service only eight years earlier, he was quickly able to find the address. The tiny "house" was at street level but was embedded into the hillside, like an ancient cave or grotto. We waited in the taxi while he knocked at the door and then spoke to the man who answered. He handed him the letter. The man became visibly excited and then disappeared inside the house. Then reappearing, he and the driver hurried to the car to welcome us and eagerly brought us into his home. This was the father, worn and weary and spiritless. He must have once been a tall and handsome man but he seems now resigned to his destiny, with tired brown eyes, graying hair and a large, unkempt white mustache accenting his unshaven face. But now, with our unexpected visit, he has become energized.

The front room was small and dark, illuminated only by the small window next to the door. Behind the front room were a few dark recesses, presumably other rooms, windowless. We were invited to sit as the man brought us some water. No one else was there. Language was clearly a problem because neither the man nor the driver spoke or understood English. After he and the driver talked for several minutes, the driver left the little house, apparently on an errand. Nadene and I, together with our host, were eager to communicate but could only sit silently and uncomfortably, waiting. But for what?

Soon the driver returned with a burly fellow, about 60, who had returned to live out the rest of his years in his home town after 40 years of growing rich in Tchi-cah-go! And now, to his prideful gratification, he was the village's widely admired and respected Big Shot. He seemed a decent fellow and was dressed, as always, in a suit and tie, and was genial and excited by our visit. And he was the welcome needed link for communication. So the five of us began to engage, with the father endlessly asking me many questions about his son. Even the driver, who remembers the son, joined the conversation.

But something was missing. Finally Nadene asked about the mother, and after an awkward pause was told she was still in the back and not supposed to be involved. Mr. Tchi-cah-go intervened and explained a few things to father, who then went into the deep shadows and brought out mother. She had been told of our presence and the contents of the letter but was not permitted to come out to welcome us. She was a small woman, aged beyond her years, and appeared a little bewildered by this breakdown of her customary place in the traditional hierarchy. Nadene and I were there for about an hour and were able to answer so many questions. As I described what life was like in San Diego for a student at the University, mother and father sat in quiet astonishment. Yet there it all was, a mother's tears and a father's pride.

Father, in his exuberance declared that we should all go up onto the next street and visit the village taverna to share his wonderful news with his friends. Of course mother was not included because women are traditionally excluded. But Nadene would be a special exception. So mother remained in her solitude in the cave while Nadene and I, the driver, father and Mr. Tchi-cah-go walked up to the taverna. The room was crowded and boisterous and as we walked in all the patrons suddenly fell silent at lovely Nadene's presence. But Mr. Tchi-cah-go explained everything. We were then seated at a table and con-tinuously plied with ouzo and delicious delicacies of who knows what and ouzo and more mysterious edibles and more ouzo. Curious and admiring men came to the table for introductions. And father was in his element expressing his pride in the accomplishments of his son. After a spirited hour and with Mr. Tchi-cah-go's help we thanked our hosts, bade farewell and left this unforgettable taverna.

With an embracing goodbye to father and Mr. Tchi-cah-go we were about to drive off when mother came out of the house and quickly ran to the taxi. With tears of gratitude she handed us two ripe plump oranges, a rare, hoarded treasure in a village like this. I reached through the car window and through my own tears felt the anguish and thankfulness in her eyes as I held her hand so tenderly.

LEN VEITZER October 2013

.... INTO THE WILD BLUE YONDER

For my 75th birthday my son Jason flew down to San Diego from San Francisco to present me with a wonderful and unexpected surprise. Always aware and sensitive to my passionate lifelong interest in airplanes and flying, he had made reservations for me at Mcclellan-Palomar Airport (just east of Carlsbad) to fly with a pilot in a vintage World War 2 fighter training plane, the most advanced trainer a cadet flies prior to earning his wings.

But before Mcclellan we drove up the I-215 to March Air Force Base in Riverside County to visit the March Field Museum with indoor and outdoor exhibits of WW2 and current combat aircraft. Among the vintage planes are B-17s (Flying Fortress), B-25s (Billy Mitchell), B-29s (Superfortress), and classic fighter planes like the P-38 Lightning, the P-51 Mustang as well as many, many more. The museum is not unlike San Diego's Air and Space museum in Balboa Park. For most people this redundancy might be a little excessive but as for me, I can't get enough of it. And Jason knows that and that's why we're here.

Later when we checked in at the Mcclellan-Palomar Airport the beautifully restored North American T-6 Texan was parked on the tarmac seemingly happy to be waiting for me.

The T-6 is a two-place advanced trainer that was the classroom for most of the Allied pilots who flew in World War 2. Called the SNJ by the Navy and the Harvard by the British Royal Air Force, the advanced trainer T-6 was designed as a transition trainer between basic trainers and first-line tactical aircraft. In all, the T-6 trained several hundred thousand pilots in 34 different countries over a period of 25 years. A total of 15,495 of the planes were made.

Jason and I went out to meet the pilot, who was doing a pre-flight inspection. He and I mounted the plane and climbed into our seats. He was in the front cockpit of the tandem arrangement and I was in the back. He led me through all the command protocols and commun-nication techniques. I was absolutely thrilled and excited. How many years (decades) had I dreamed about this. My first impression, apropos of nothing, was that the 550 horsepower engine was very, very loud. We taxied to the end of the runway, turned about, and roared down the runway heading west toward the Pacific. Gaining altitude as we crossed the shoreline, the pilot made a broad sweeping right turn northward, continuing into the u-turn until we were heading east and climbing past 2,000 feet. The sky was clear and bright and as I looked below could make out landmarks I was familiar with on the ground. We crossed the I-15 continuing our climb. Soon the I-805 passed below us and by now we were at 6,000 feet. And the pilot said to me, "are you ready to fly?"

Boy was I, and he handed over control. He had me bank left and then right, climb to 6,500 feet and then dive to 4,000. "Are you up for a barrel roll?" he asked. He knew I was and directed me to climb back up to 5,000 feet. I handed over control and he performed a beautiful and graceful horizontal barrel roll. Then he suggested a loop. I said "sure" and he gunned the engine to full throttle, dived to pick up speed, pulled back the stick and began a vertical climb that became a loop. It was a new sensation to me to watch the horizon slipping away below us and then nothing but blue sky in front of us. Soon the horizon reappeared from above as we leveled out. I was exhilarated!

Now we're back at 5,000 and I'm in control, banking left and then right. Then on his command I make a right turn and continue south for a few miles, a left turn and rise to 6,000 feet, and another right turn. I've gotten comfortable with the controls and the basic maneuvers and feel the rhythm of flying. It all seems to me so natural.

Suddenly the pilot says to me, "See that plane down there?" And yes there is another plane about 500 feet below and ahead of us flying in the same direction. And the pilot in a playful voice says "Let's go get 'im!" When I hand over control, he peels off to the left and dives down to be on the tail of this other plane. With a mischievous cackle he presses a button on his control panel and a mock machine gun sound, rat-atat-tat, rat-atat-tat rattles in our ears. "We got 'im," he chuckles as we pull up triumphantly, turn around and he puts me in control as we head back toward the coast. After about an hour of flying this morning we get close to the airport and he takes control and lands the airplane. As we taxi toward the hangar Jason is waiting for me, with open arms and a wide loving smile on his dear face. And I thought about how, in spite of my instincts and desires, my introduction to flying was delayed from my youth until now. And I'm forever grateful to Jason for helping me to close my circle.

LEN VEITZER
May 2018

JASON ERIC VEITZER

AUGUST 1, 1967 -- MARCH 14, 2018

Dear Lord

Thank you for providing me with a life of joy and peace.

Thank you for delivering me with the opportunity to live a full life.

Thank you for surrounding me with caring friends and a loving family.

Take me when you will
Take me where you will
Take me as you will

One lifetime
Thank you Lord.

Jason